The Galápagos Islands

90°W

rchena
OLOE

Genovesa
TOWER

Equator

Galápagos

N

0   10   20   30   40   50

Km

ur

✈ **Baltra**
SOUTH SEYMOUR

○ **Plazas**

Santa Cruz
INDEFATIGABLE

Charles
Darwin
Research
Station

Santa Fé
BARRINGTON

**PUERTO
BAQUERIZO
MORENO**

San Cristóbal
CHATHAM

Iderby
ampion

Caldwell
○ **Gardner**
○ **Watson**

Española
HOOD

Gardner

Birds, Mammals, & Reptiles of the Galápagos Islands

Birds, Mammals, & Reptiles of the Galápagos Islands

An identification guide

Andy Swash and Rob Still

With illustrations by Ian Lewington

First published 2000 by Pica Press and **WILD**_Guides_
and in the United States by Yale University Press.

Second Edition published 2005 by Christopher Helm,
an imprint of A&C Black Publishers Ltd., 36 Soho Square,
London W1D 3QY and **WILD**_Guides_ Ltd., Parr House,
63 Hatch Lane, Old Basing, Hampshire RG24 7EB and in
the United States by Yale University Press.

Reprinted 2007

© 2000 and 2005 Andy Swash and Rob Still (text and maps),
© 2000 and 2005 Ian Lewington, Marc Dando and Rob Still
(illustrations)
Copyright in the photographs remains with the individual
photographers.

Library of Congress Control Number: 2005930975

ISBN-13: 978-0-300-11532-1

A CIP catalogue record for this book is available from the British Library.

This book is produced using paper that is made from wood
grown in managed sustainable forests. It is natural, renewable
and recyclable. The logging and manufacturing processes
conform to the environmental regulations of the country
of origin.

www.acblack.com
www.wildguides.co.uk
www.yalebooks.com

Production and design by **WILD**_Guides_, Old Basing, Hampshire.
Printed and bound in China via 1010 Printing International Ltd.

10   9   8   7   6   5   4

CONTENTS

FOREWORD

Until the discovery of the Islands in 1535, the flora and fauna of Galápagos evolved in isolation, producing strange and marvellous island species, as Charles Darwin found when he visited the islands 300 years later. Nowadays many people can and do visit the islands to see the unique wildlife. One of the most remarkable things about Galápagos is that today's visitor can still encounter almost all the species that were present when Darwin and his predecessors came here. This is in striking contrast to the catastrophic chains of extinctions that have occurred in every other large oceanic archipelago following the arrival of man.

Modern visitors to Galápagos come to experience the wildlife and the lava landscapes and are invariably keen to identify the species they encounter. In many cases this experience fuels a desire to learn more about the relationships between the plants and animals and their environment. Such curiosity is amply rewarded when observing the thoroughly approachable, sometimes almost nonchalant Galápagos wildlife.

For many people, field guides provide the first insight into the diversity of wildlife and the intricacies and complexities of the natural world. This compact, well thought out and clearly presented book provides a comprehensive guide to the terrestrial vertebrates found in Galápagos. It is simple to use, the text is concise and the innovative use of digital technology has produced a remarkable collection of plates. An informative guide of this kind will help everyone from beginner to experienced naturalist.

With its ecological message – and the publisher's generous commitment to make a donation to the Charles Darwin Research Station for every copy sold – this book will also help conserve the Islands' wildlife. With over 15,000 people resident in the islands, daily flights, regular cargo boats from the mainland, and increasing local fishing pressure, the Islands no longer offer a safe, isolated haven to the vulnerable, endemic plants and animals. However, the Station, together with the Galápagos National Park Service, are working with skill and dedication to ensure that the encroachment of the modern world upon Galápagos is controlled and that the wildlife will continue to flourish. If you want to know more about our conservation, research and education work, or about the worldwide "Friends of Galápagos" network, then please visit our website at www. galapagos.org. I hope that this fine field guide will inspire you both to observe and to preserve the wonderful wildlife of Galápagos.

[signature]

Dr Robert Bensted-Smith
Director
Charles Darwin Research Station

ACKNOWLEDGEMENTS

Many people have contributed to the production of this book and our sincere thanks are due to them all. It is our intention that everyone who has contributed to the book is named in this section, but if we have inadvertently missed anyone we can only apologise. Despite the contributions of others, we hold full responsibility for any errors which may have crept in, and for any omissions which may have been made.

With our limited knowledge of cetaceans, we would not have been able to write a definitive guide to the identification of the many species which have been recorded in Galápagos. We are, therefore, particularly indebted to Dylan Walker for his very significant contribution in writing this part of the book, and for collating the photographs which appear on the plates.

Condensing the plethora of information available on the birds of Galápagos, and defining their key identification features, proved to be particularly time-consuming and we are extremely grateful to Richard Kershaw for his tremendous assistance in helping to complete this task.

The plates are one of the key features of the book and are based largely on photographs taken by photographers from throughout the world. We would like to acknowledge the skill and patience of the following photographers who kindly allowed us to include their work in the book: Charles Anderson, Nigel Bean, Giff Beaton, Carla Benoldi, Alex Carlisle, Kevin Carlson, Colin Carver, Roger Charlwood, John Cooper, David Cottridge, Graeme Cresswell, Yvonne Dean, Paul Doherty, Robert Dowler, Cody W. Edwards, Paul Ellis, Tom Ennis, Dagmar C. Fertl, John Geeson, Michael Gore, Bruce Hallett, Phil Hansbro, Hugh Harrop, Matt Hobbs, Brayton Holt, David Horwell, Barry Hughes, Boris Klusmeyer/Global Gecko Association, Gordon Langsbury, Tim Loseby, Mark Lucas, George McCallum/Whalephoto Berlin, Colin McLeod, Gary McCracken, Tony Marr, Lori Mazzuca, Jonathan Mitchell, Arthur Morris, Simon Mustoe, Phil Myers/Animal Diversity Web, Dirk Neumann, Philip Newbold, Dick Newell, Howard Nicholls, Stephanie A. Norman, Dave Nye, Tony Palliser, Pietro Pecchioni, Robert L. Pitman, Mark Rauzon, Richard Revels, Chris Schenk, Hadoram Shirihai, Howard and Heidi Snell, Peggy Stap, Gill Swash, Alan Tate, Sam Taylor, David Tipling, Ralph Todd, Dylan Walker, Stephen Wong, Steve Young. The name of the photographer who took each photograph is shown in the photographic credits section of this book which starts on page 157. We would especially like to thank David Tipling of Windrush Photographs for his help in obtaining high quality photographs of some of the particularly difficult bird species, and to Tony Hutson for help with the bats.

Whilst we had originally intended to illustrate the book entirely with photographs, we were unable to source images of sufficiently high quality of all the species. There are very few illustrators who have the ability to paint birds accurately and make them appear lifelike: this was the reason for our wishing to use photographs in the first place. In our opinion, one of the best bird illustrators in the business is Ian Lewington and we were therefore delighted that he agreed to paint the plate of hirundines and Chimney Swift in flight (Plate 29), the measured drawings of the beaks of the Darwin's Finches (Plate 34) and the few 'missing' birds on the remaining plates. In this respect, we are also grateful to The Natural History Museum, Tring for allowing access to study the bird skins in their collection. Thanks are also due to Marc Dando for allowing us to use some of his artwork for the introduction to the cetaceans section and one of the plates.

Mavis and Len Still helped to type and format first drafts of much of the text. Robert Brooks, Mary Swash Brooks and Richard Kershaw kindly proof-read the text at an early stage and Nigel Redman undertook the final edit of the book; all provided very helpful comments.

Thanks are also due to Mike Lindley and Sally-Ann Wilson for their help in sourcing reference material for the reptile section, to Amanda Hillier and Diana Langley of the Galápagos Conservation Trust, Howard and Heidi Snell at the Charles Darwin Research Station, Paul Coopmans, Hernan Vargas and Marco Altamirano for their help with various last-minute queries.

We are delighted that Rob Bensted-Smith, the Director of the CDRS, agreed to write the Foreword to the book, and are most grateful for his kind words.

Lastly, but by no means least, our wives, Gill and Penny, deserve special mention for their help, patience and understanding during the production of the book.

INTRODUCTION

About this book

This book aims to provide a handy yet comprehensive field guide to help visitors to Galápagos identify with confidence any bird, mammal or reptile they encounter.

The book focuses on the key identification features which separate each species from all others, highlighting where necessary the differences between males and females, and, in the case of birds, the different plumages. Summary information is provided on each species' status and habitat preferences and, where appropriate, behavioural characteristics and breeding seasons.

Each of the extant species of bird, mammal and reptile which has ever been recorded in Galápagos is covered, and all, bar a few of the lava lizards and leaf-toed geckos which are confined to single islands, are illustrated with photographs or paintings. The plates which form the bulk of the book are based on digitally manipulated images which have been resized to ensure that the species on each plate are in proportion.

We have chosen to be comprehensive in the coverage of the species in order to help visitors to the islands record all the species they see; it would be very easy to dismiss sightings of unusual species simply because they are not covered. We hope that by illustrating or describing them all (and in the case of birds their various plumages), visitors will be better able to contribute to the scientific record by submitting details of their sightings to the relevant authority. The Charles Darwin Research Station welcomes records of all scarce residents or migrants and vagrants. Details should be sent, including as full a description as possible, to the CDRS (see page 156 for contact details).

It is beyond the scope of this book to provide detailed information on the biology or ecology of each of the species, since such information is readily available in the many excellent books which have been published already on the wildlife of Galápagos. This book is an identification guide which we hope will stimulate further reading once the observer is confident of the identity of the birds, mammals and reptiles he or she encounters whilst exploring these fascinating islands.

How to use this book

The book is divided into seven main sections. The following two sections give a brief overview of the geography and climate (pages 10–11) and the habitats of Galápagos (pages 12–16), and emphasise the key factors that influence the distribution and breeding strategies of species in the archipelago.

The bulk of the book comprises stand-alone sections on the birds (pages 17–109), reptiles (pages 110–125) and mammals (pages 126–149). The first part of each of these sections provides an introduction to the 'types' of species that occur in Galápagos. This is followed by a series of plates, each with an accompanying page of text that summarises the status of each of the species shown and highlights the key identification features.

The final section of the book includes a checklist of the resident and regularly occurring species which summarises their habitat preferences and distribution (pages 150–154), a glossary of technical terms (page 155), suggestions for further reading (page 156), and a list of all the photographs and illustrations used in the book (pages 157–164).

THE GEOGRAPHY AND CLIMATE OF GALÁPAGOS

Geography

The Galápagos Islands are volcanic in origin and situated in the Pacific Ocean, straddling the equator, about 960km west of Ecuador in mainland South America and 1,100km from Costa Rica in Central America. The total land area of the archipelago is 7,882km² and the coastline extends to 1,336km.

The distance from the island of Darwin in the north-west to Española in the south-east is 430km; and it is 220km from Punta Cristóbal, the south-westernmost point of Isabela, to Genovesa in the north-east.

Nineteen of the islands have a surface area of over 1km² and 13 are over 10km². In addition, there are 42 islets with a surface area of less than 1km² and 26 emerging rocks. The largest island, Isabela, extends to 4,588km², representing over 70% of the land area. The highest point in Galápagos is Volcan Wolf on Isabela, which rises to 1,707m. The size and highest point of each of the main islands is shown in the following table. Five of the islands are inhabited and the resident population is approaching 17,000.

Island	Area (km²)	Altitude (m)	Inhabited
Isabela	4,588	1,707	Yes
Santa Cruz	986	864	Yes
Fernandina	642	1,494	No
Santiago	585	907	No
San Cristóbal	558	730	Yes
Floreana	173	640	Yes
Marchena	130	343	No
Española	60	206	No
Pinta	60	777	No
Baltra	27	100	Yes
Santa Fé	24	259	No
Pinzón	18	458	No
Genovesa	14	76	No
Rábida	4.9	367	No
Seymour	1.9	–	No
Wolf	1.3	253	No
Tortuga	1.2	186	No
Bartolomé	1.2	114	No
Darwin	1.1	168	No

Climate

The climate of Galápagos is unusually dry for the tropics, although there are considerable differences between the islands and much annual variation. However, there are two distinct seasons: the warm/wet season (December to May) and the Garúa (misty) or dry season (May to December). During the warm/wet season the skies are usually clear and the temperature can exceed 30ºC, although it is humid and heavy rains occur. The Garúa season brings a subtropical climate, with the higher parts of the main islands often clothed in cloud for days on end. The direction of the prevailing south-easterly and north-easterly tradewinds means that the rainfall is concentrated on the southern and eastern slopes of the higher islands, the northern and western slopes being drier.

The average monthly temperatures (maximum and minimum), rainfall, and hours of sunshine are shown in the graphs opposite.

A number of ocean currents converge in Galápagos and these have a direct influence on the climate. The currents include the cold Peru Coastal (or Humboldt) and Peru Oceanic Currents from the south, driven by the south-easterly tradewinds, and the warm Niño (or Panamá) Flow from the north, which is driven by the north-easterly tradewinds. These join the South Equatorial Current which passes the islands in a westerly direction. To the west of the archipelago this

Average maximum and minimum monthly temperatures (°C)

Average monthly rainfall (mm) and hours of sunshine

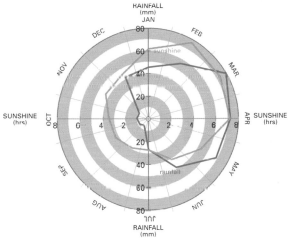

meets the cold, easterly-flowing Cromwell Current (or Equatorial Undercurrent) creating an upwelling that provides a rich source of food for many of the seabirds and marine mammals that occur in Galápagos. The timing of this upwelling is rather unpredictable and, as a consequence, many of the breeding species do so opportunistically.

In some years (on average one year in seven), the relative flow of warm currents is much greater than usual, resulting in an El Niño event. During such events, the surface temperature of the sea is much higher than usual and there is a very considerable increase in rainfall. This results in the rapid growth of vegetation and an increase in the populations of many of the landbirds. However, El Niño events also suppress the upwelling of cold waters, reducing the amount of food available for seabirds and marine mammals, the result of which is usually a significant decline in the populations of these species.

THE HABITATS OF GALÁPAGOS

The habitats of Galápagos can be divided into eight types, including the open sea and rocky islets. Six distinct vegetation zones are generally recognised which are broadly defined by altitude, reflecting the pattern of rainfall. Whilst these vegetation zones do differ from island to island, they are useful in describing the types of habitat in which the different species of birds and animals are found. The three vegetation zones which occur at the highest altitude are sometimes treated as one and termed the humid 'zone'. The term 'highlands' is used in this book to encompass all the vegetation zones from the transition zone upwards.

The open sea

The highly productive waters of Galápagos provide food for vast numbers of seabirds, as well as many species of cetacean (whales and dolphins). Some of the seabirds occur well away from land when they are feeding.

Seabird feeding frenzy – off Roca Redonda

Rocky islets

There are many sparsely vegetated rocky islets in Galápagos archipelago. The larger of these provide nesting sites for seabirds and some are home to Marine Iguanas and lava lizards.

Rocky islet – Roca Redonda

Seabird colony – Genovesa

The shore zone

The shore (or littoral) zone encompasses the range of habitats that occur close to the sea, including salt-water lagoons. These habitats include rocky shores, sea cliffs, sandy beaches and lagoons, as well as areas of mangroves, saltbush and Sea Purslane *Sesuvium* which are able to tolerate the saline conditions. The habitats of the shore zone support many seabirds, waterbirds and shorebirds as well some landbirds. The most obvious mammalian inhabitants are the sea lions, and the shore zone is also home to Marine Iguanas and turtles. In addition, lava lizards and leaf-toed geckos are found here, and snakes can occasionally be seen.

Rocky shore – Fernandina

Sandy beach and mangroves – Black Beach, Isabela

Mangroves – Turtle Cove, Santa Cruz

Lagoon bordered by saltbush – Rábida

The arid zone

The arid zone is the most diverse and extensive of all the vegetation zones in Galápagos. It occurs in the lowlands, extending inland from the shore zone, and is found on all of the main islands. The habitats that are typical of this zone include plant communities characterised by the presence of cacti and deciduous trees such as Palo Santo, Palo Verde and acacias. These habitats are home to virtually all of the species of landbird and also provide nesting sites for some of the seabirds, such as boobies and storm-petrels. Many of the reptiles, notably lava lizards and land iguanas, are at their most numerous in this zone, and rice rats also occur.

Prickly Pear cactus Opuntia *and Sea Purslane* Sesuvium *– South Plaza*

Palo Santo trees during the dry season – Isabela

The transition zone

The transition zone is characterised by a reduced number of the trees and shrubs which are typical of the arid zone and the presence of lichens and perennial herbs. The soils in this area are deeper than in the arid zone and the rainfall is higher. Most of the agricultural areas occur in the transition zone, with cattle grazing being the dominant form of land use. Many of the landbirds occur in this zone, as do Galápagos (or Giant) Tortoises.

Transition zone, agricultural area   Santa Cruz

Transition zone, disused agricultural area – Floreana

The humid 'zone'

The term humid 'zone' is often used to encompass the three distinct broad vegetation types that occur in the higher parts of the larger islands. These are the Scalezia, Miconia and pampa zones; a brief description of each follows.

The *Scalezia* zone

On the larger, higher islands the transition zone gives way to a moist, lush cloud-forest-type vegetation which consists of dense shrubs dominated by *Scalezia* trees. These trees, which are endemic to Galápagos, can reach a height of almost 20 metres and are festooned with mosses, liverworts, ferns, bromeliads and orchids. The *Scalezia* zone supports many species of landbird and provides breeding sites for the Dark-rumped Petrel.

The Miconia zone

The very wet, high altitude *Miconia* zone is found only on the southern slopes of Santa Cruz and San Cristóbal. It is treeless and occurs above the *Scalezia* zone, being characterised by dense stands of the endemic Miconia shrub, which grows to about two metres. Many species of grasses, liverworts and ferns are present in this zone which, due to its wetness, supports only a few species of landbirds.

The pampa zone

The pampa zone is the highest and wettest vegetation zone in Galápagos, usually occurring above 500 metres. Dominated by grasses, sedges and ferns, including the Galápagos Tree Fern that can grow to about three metres, the prevailing damp conditions mean that few species of birds, other than the ground-dwelling rails, are able to thrive.

Scalezia *zone – Santa Cruz*

Pampa zone – Isabela

THE BIRDS OF GALÁPAGOS

Introduction

In total, 154 bird species have been recorded in Galápagos. Only 61 of these are resident, although 29 are endemic to Galápagos (i.e. they are found nowhere else on earth) and a further 15 are represented by endemic subspecies. The other 93 species are either migrants that occur at least annually (25 species) or vagrants (68 species).

The species can be divided into eight 'types' which broadly reflect the habitats in which they occur. The following table lists these types and provides a summary of the number of species recorded and their status.

Type	Species Recorded	Status			Endemic Species	Endemic Subspecies
		Residents	Migrants	Vagrants		
Seabirds	48	19	4	25	6	7
Waterbirds	23	11	1	11	2	3
Shorebirds	34	2	16	16		1
Diurnal raptors	3	1	2		1	
Nightbirds	3	2		1		2
Larger landbirds	8	5	1	2	1	
Aerial feeders	6	1	1	4	1	
Smaller landbirds	29	20		9	18	2

It is a sad fact that seven of the resident species of Galápagos are threatened with extinction. Standard criteria for categorising the degree of threat that species face have been adopted by The International Union for Conservation of Nature and Natural Resources (the World Conservation Union) (IUCN). A summary of the definitions of these categories, and the species which are considered to fall into each, are shown in the following table.

Category	Definition	Galápagos species concerned
CRITICALLY ENDANGERED	Facing an extremely high risk of extinction in the wild in the immediate future.	Dark-rumped Petrel Mangrove Finch
ENDANGERED	Not critical but facing a very high risk of extinction in the wild in the immediate future.	Charles Mockingbird
VULNERABLE	Not endangered but facing a high risk of extinction in the wild in the medium-term future.	Galápagos Penguin Flightless Cormorant Galápagos Hawk Lava Gull

In addition, Elliot's Storm-petrel is considered to be **DATA DEFICIENT** (which means that inadequate information is available to assess the risk of extinction) and Waved Albatross, Wedge-rumped Storm-petrel, Galápagos Rail and Medium Tree Finch are considered **NEAR-THREATENED** (which means that, although they are at little risk of extinction in the medium-term future, they are still of conservation concern).

Bird topography

It is helpful to have some knowledge of the structure of a bird, and the names of the various parts, when attempting to identify a species and/or describe its features. For some species the colour or patterns of different groups of feathers can be particularly important in identification, and a knowledge of their arrangement is therefore also useful. The terms used in this book for the various parts of a bird, and the arrangement of the main feather tracts, are shown on the following photographs of Swallow-tailed Gull, Semipalmated Plover, Large Ground Finch and Chatham Mockingbird.

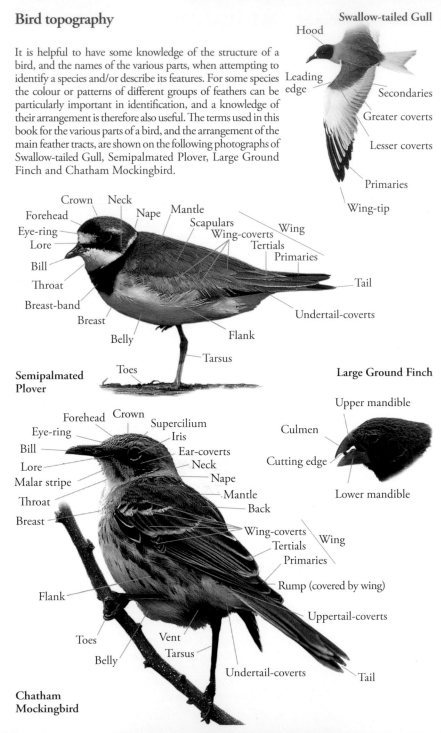

Swallow-tailed Gull

Hood
Leading edge
Secondaries
Greater coverts
Lesser coverts
Primaries
Wing-tip

Crown Neck
Forehead Nape Mantle
Eye-ring Scapulars
Lore Wing-coverts Wing
Bill Tertials
Throat Primaries
Breast-band
Breast Tail
Belly Undertail-coverts
Tarsus Flank
Toes

Semipalmated Plover

Large Ground Finch

Upper mandible
Culmen
Cutting edge
Lower mandible

Forehead Crown
Eye-ring Supercilium
Bill Iris
Lore Ear-coverts
Malar stripe Neck
Throat Nape
Breast Mantle
Back
Wing-coverts Wing
Tertials
Primaries
Flank Rump (covered by wing)
Uppertail-coverts
Toes Vent
Belly Tarsus
Undertail-coverts Tail

Chatham Mockingbird

Moult and plumages

All birds replace their feathers – termed moult – at least once a year, the plumage often changing with successive moults. Some knowledge of the moult strategies of the different types of bird is therefore essential to the correct ageing of individuals, and in some cases is an invaluable aid to identification. Although moult strategies can be complex, most of the species within the groups of birds covered by this book follow a similar pattern. A summary of the sequences of plumages which occur is given in this section. In the New World, a different terminology is generally applied, and these alternatives are given in square brackets.

Juvenile [Juvenal] plumage
Juvenile plumage is the first plumage a bird attains once it has lost its down. In many species, juvenile plumage is very different from subsequent plumages. The juvenile feathers of many passerines have a rather 'loose' structure which often gives the bird a fluffy appearance. Most birds moult their juvenile feathers quite quickly after fledging and attain *first-winter* [*first basic*] plumage.

First-winter [First basic] plumage
First-winter plumage is the term used to describe the plumage most shorebirds, gulls and passerines attain after their first (post-*juvenile* [*first pre-basic*]) moult. During this moult it is usually only the body feathers which are replaced; the juvenile flight and tail feathers being retained (i.e. a *partial moult*). This can result in a distinctive plumage, notably in gulls.

First-summer [First alternate] plumage
Most species undergo a *pre-breeding* [*first pre-alternate*] *moult* during which at least some of the body feathers are replaced. This results in recognisable first-summer plumages with most shorebirds, gulls and passerines.

First adult [First definitive] plumage
Some birds, including pigeons and doves, undergo a *post-juvenile* [*first pre-basic*] *moult* during which all the feathers are replaced (i.e. a *complete moult*) and are subsequently inseparable from adults.

Subsequent immature plumages
A few species occurring in Galápagos take a number of years to attain adult plumage (e.g. certain gulls). These often have distinguishable immature plumages which chronologically are termed *second-winter* [*second basic*], *second-summer* [*second alternate*], and *third-winter* [*third basic*].

Adult [Definitive] plumage
Adult plumage is the final plumage a bird attains once it has reached maturity. Many species have just one adult plumage which is retained throughout the year, although others, notably the ducks, gulls and shorebirds, have different breeding [alternate] and non-breeding [basic] plumages. Adult birds adopt one of four moult strategies, depending upon the species, and this generally determines the differences between breeding and non-breeding plumages.

- *One complete post-breeding [pre-basic] moult per year* – e.g. most seabirds, diurnal (day-flying) raptors, nightbirds, pigeons and doves, and swifts.
- *One complete post-breeding [pre-basic] moult per year and a pre-breeding [pre-alternate] partial moult* – e.g. gulls, terns, skuas and jaegers, ducks, herons and egrets.
- *A partial post-breeding [pre-basic] moult and a complete pre-breeding [pre-alternate] moult* – some long-distance migrant passerines.
- *Two complete moults per year* – the only species recorded in Galápagos which are known to adopt this strategy are Franklin's Gull and Bobolink.

The types of bird

This part of the book provides an introduction to each of the eight 'types' of bird that occur in Galápagos and aims to aid initial identification. Each of these 'types' can be further subdivided into groups (which broadly equate to Families) and the following sections provide a description of each. The text for each group is cross-referenced to the relevant plate(s) which illustrate all the species ever to have been recorded. The species and subspecies within each group which are endemic to Galápagos are listed, the names of endemic species being shown in UPPER CASE text.

SEABIRDS

In total, 48 species of seabird have been recorded in Galápagos, 19 of which are resident. The seabirds therefore account for nearly one third of all the species ever recorded in the islands and about the same proportion of the resident species.

The seabirds can be conveniently divided into 12 groups, as shown in the following table. This shows the number of species recorded in each group and summarises their status. It also shows the number of endemic species and the number of other species which are represented by endemic subspecies. Species are treated as migrants if they occur annually, vagrants being those recorded less frequently.

Group (Plate No.)	Species Recorded	Status			Endemic Species	Endemic Subspecies
		Residents	Migrants	Vagrants		
Penguins (1)	1	1			1	
Cormorants (1)	1	1			1	
Pelicans (1)	1	1				1
Albatrosses (2)	4	1		3	1	
Shearwaters and petrels (2–4)	12	2	1	9	1	1
Storm-petrels (5–6)	8	3	1	4		2
Frigatebirds (7)	2	2				1
Boobies (8)	4	3		1		1
Skuas and jaegers (9)	2			2		
Gulls (9–10)	6	2	2	2	2	
Terns (11–12)	6	2		4		1
Tropicbirds (11)	1	1				
Total:	47	19	4	24	6	7

Galápagos Penguin (adult)

PENGUINS   Family: Spheniscidae
1 species recorded (resident)   (Plate 1)

Endemic species: GALÁPAGOS PENGUIN

Penguins are flightless, marine birds with thickset bodies; short, robust legs with webbed feet; and stout bills. The wings are compressed to form powerful, rigid flippers that are used for swimming underwater. When they are in the water, penguins can be difficult to see, as even when they are on the surface their bodies are held very low, often with only the head and neck visible. On land they appear rather clumsy, standing upright and walking with a waddling gait and occasional hops. The sexes are alike.

Flightless Cormorant (adult)

CORMORANTS
1 species recorded (resident)

Family: Phalacrocoracidae
(Plate 1)

Endemic species: FLIGHTLESS (or GALÁPAGOS) CORMORANT

Cormorants are largish waterbirds with elongated bodies; short, set-back legs with large, webbed feet; long necks; and long, hooked bills which are used to catch fish underwater. Cormorants can be difficult to see when they are in the water as even when they are on the surface they hold their body low, sometimes with only the head and neck showing. On land, they are rather ungainly, walking slowly and methodically. After returning to land from a period of feeding at sea they habitually hold their wings out to dry. The Flightless (or Galápagos) Cormorant is the largest and only flightless cormorant in the world. The sexes are alike and immature plumages resemble adult plumage.

Brown Pelican (adult)

PELICANS
1 species recorded (resident)

Family: Pelecanidae
(Plate 1)

Endemic subspecies: Brown Pelican

Pelicans are large, heavy waterbirds with short legs, webbed feet and exceptionally long bills. The bill has a large, distensible pouch which is used as a scoop-net to catch fish. In flight, pelicans hold their head and neck drawn back and have slow, rather ponderous wingbeats; they are, however, accomplished gliders. Pelicans are very ungainly on land, rarely walking far. The sexes are alike.

Waved Albatross (adult)

ALBATROSSES
4 species recorded (1 resident; 3 vagrants)

Family: Diomedeidae
(Plate 2)

Endemic species: WAVED ALBATROSS

Albatrosses are the largest of the seabirds, with extremely long, narrow wings which are held stiffly in flight. They have long, stout, hook-tipped bills with raised tubular nostrils, and shortish legs with large, webbed feet. Albatrosses are exceptional gliders, rarely flapping their wings other than in calm conditions. During such conditions they often sit on the sea for long periods. Albatrosses only come to land to breed and when they do they are somewhat ungainly, walking with a slow, rather waddling gait. The sexes are alike. The immature plumages of the Waved Albatross resemble the adult plumage (this is not the case with the other species recorded as vagrants to Galápagos).

Galápagos Shearwater (adult)

SHEARWATERS and PETRELS
12 species recorded
(2 residents; 1 migrant; 9 vagrants)

Family: Procellariidae
(Plates 2–4)

Endemic species: GALÁPAGOS SHEARWATER

Endemic subspecies: Dark-rumped Petrel

Although the species in the family Procellariidae range from the large giant petrels to the diminutive prions (which have both been recorded as vagrants to Galápagos), the species which are recorded regularly can be divided into two groups: shearwaters and petrels. All species in the family are long-winged, have short legs and webbed feet, and raised nostril

21

Dark-rumped Petrel (adult)

tubes at the base of the bill. Shearwaters are medium-sized, rather compact seabirds with long, slender bills and straight, stiffly-held wings in flight. Petrels are similar in size and shape to shearwaters but, in comparison, have short, deep bills and in flight tend to hold their wings slightly forward from the shoulder and sharply angled at the wrist or carpal joint. In all species recorded in Galápagos the sexes are alike and immature plumages resemble adult plumage.

Elliot's Storm-petrel (adult)

STORM-PETRELS
Family: Hydrobatidae
8 species recorded
(Plates 5–6)
(3 residents; 1 migrant; 4 vagrants)

Endemic subspecies: Wedge-rumped Storm-petrel; Elliot's (or White-vented) Storm-petrel

Storm-petrels are the smallest of the seabirds with tube-noses (raised nostril-tubes at the base of the bill). They have short to medium-length wings in proportion to their size and usually fly close to the sea with a characteristic gliding flight action interspersed with rapid wingbeats. Storm-petrels have longish legs and webbed feet, and the species most likely to be seen in Galápagos are dark with white rumps. The sexes of all species recorded in Galápagos are alike, and immature plumages resemble adult plumage.

FRIGATEBIRDS
Family: Fregatidae
2 species recorded (both resident)
(Plate 7)
Endemic subspecies: Magnificent Frigatebird

Magnificent Frigatebird (adult male)

Frigatebirds are large, dark seabirds with very long, pointed wings which are held forward from the shoulder in flight. They have deeply forked tails and short legs with webbed feet. Their bills are long and hook-tipped. Frigatebirds soar high over the sea and feed by harassing and kleptoparasitising other seabirds, particularly boobies, or by picking food from the surface of the sea. However, they never land on water. The male, female and immature plumages are distinctly different and breeding males have a bright red gular pouch which is inflated during display.

BOOBIES
Family: Sulidae
4 species recorded (3 residents; 1 vagrant)
(Plate 8)
Endemic subspecies: Blue-footed Booby

Nazca Booby (adult)

Boobies are large, conspicuous seabirds with cigar-shaped bodies, long dagger-shaped bills and, in flight, long pointed wings and characteristic wedge-shaped tails. They have rather short legs but large webbed feet which, in the case of the Blue-footed and Red-footed Boobies, are used during courtship, the birds deliberately lifting their feet and showing them to their mates. The sexes are alike. Boobies feed at sea by plunge-diving from the air.

SKUAS and JAEGERS
2 species recorded (both vagrants)

Family: Stercorariidae
(Plate 9)

Skuas and jaegers are medium-sized to largish, rather heavy-bodied, brown or brown-and-white predatory seabirds with long, pointed, angled wings (broad in the case of Catharacta skuas) and hook-tipped bills. They are reminiscent of gulls but are readily distinguished in flight in all plumages by their dark wings with white flashes at the base of the primaries. The sexes are alike.

South Polar Skua (adult)

Swallow-tailed Gull (adult and juvenile)

GULLS
6 species recorded
(2 residents; 2 migrants; 2 vagrants)

Family: Laridae
(Plates 9–10)

Endemic species: SWALLOW-TAILED GULL; LAVA GULL

Gulls are medium-sized to largish seabirds with long, pointed wings and longish, rather stout, hook-tipped bills, usually with a marked gonydeal angle. Their legs are longish and their feet webbed. The gulls recorded in Galápagos are predominantly grey and white in adult plumage, although the Lava Gull is wholly grey. The sexes are alike. Birds take a number of years to attain adult plumage and immature plumages are variable, often making identification difficult. Gulls feed by picking food from the surface of the water or by scavenging, often along the shoreline.

Common Noddy (adult)

TERNS
6 species recorded (2 residents; 4 vagrants)

Family: Sternidae
(Plates 11–12)

Endemic subspecies: Common Noddy

Terns are similar to gulls in many respects but are generally smaller, with narrower wings; thinner, straighter bills which lack the marked gonydeal angle; and shorter legs. Whilst terns are usually predominantly grey and white, the two species that breed in Galápagos are wholly dark brown (Common Noddy) and black and white (Sooty Tern). The sexes are alike. Terns feed by picking food from the surface of the water or by plunge-diving.

TROPICBIRDS
1 species recorded (resident)

Family: Phaethontidae
(Plate 11)

Tropicbirds are predominantly white seabirds, resembling gulls and terns in size and structure. They are distinguished from these birds in adult plumage by their elongated central tail feathers and in all plumages by a black 'mask' through the eye. The bill is stout and slightly decurved and the legs are short with webbed feet. The sexes are alike. Tropicbirds feed at sea, flying low over the water and plunging to catch their food. They are often seen resting on the water with the tail raised.

Red-billed Tropicbird (adult)

23

WATERBIRDS

In total, 21 species of waterbird have been recorded in Galápagos, ten of which are resident. The waterbirds can be conveniently divided into five groups, as shown in the following table. This shows the number of species recorded in each group and summarises their status. It also shows the number of endemic species and the number of other species which are represented by endemic subspecies.

| Group (Plate No.) | Species Recorded | Status | | | Endemic Species | Endemic Subspecies |
		Residents	Migrants	Vagrants		
Grebes (13)	1			1		
Ducks (13)	4	1		3		1
Rails and crakes (13,14)	6	3		3	1	
Flamingos (15)	1	1				
Herons and egrets (15–17)	11	6	1	4	1	2
Total:	22	11	1	10	2	3

Pied-billed Grebe (adult)

GREBES
Family: Podicipididae
1 species recorded (vagrant)
(Plate 13)

The only species of grebe recorded in Galápagos is the Pied-billed Grebe. This is a small, rather plump diving bird with a short neck; very short tail; straight, stout bill; and lobed toes. The sexes are alike.

White-cheeked Pintail (adults)

DUCKS
Family: Anatidae
4 species recorded (1 resident; 3 vagrants)
(Plate 13)
Endemic subspecies: White-cheeked Pintail

Ducks are medium-sized waterbirds with plump bodies, shortish necks with rounded heads, and medium-length, blunt-tipped and slightly flattened bills. Their legs are short and their feet webbed. Ducks are usually seen on the water or at rest on land. In flight, they are fast and direct, with rapid wingbeats, and the head and neck are held outstretched.

Galápagos Rail (adult)

RAILS and CRAKES
Family: Rallidae
6 species recorded (3 residents; 3 vagrants) (Plates 13–14)
Endemic species: GALÁPAGOS RAIL

Rails and crakes are small to medium-sized ground-dwelling birds with plump bodies; short tails, which are often held erect; shortish necks and bills; and long legs and toes (the feet are not webbed). They are generally rather furtive, mainly inhabiting marshy areas and are usually reluctant to fly. They are good swimmers. The sexes are alike in all species.

FLAMINGOS
Family: Phoenicopteridae
1 species recorded (resident)
(Plate 15)

Flamingos are large and unmistakable birds with extremely long legs and neck, and unique kinked bill. In adults the plumage is pink. The sexes are alike.

Greater Flamingo (adults)

HERONS and EGRETS
10 species recorded
(6 residents; 1 migrant; 4 vagrants)

Family: Ardeidae
(Plates 15–17)

Endemic species: Lava (or Galápagos) Heron

Endemic subspecies: Great Blue Heron; Yellow-crowned Night-heron

Herons, egrets and night-herons are medium- to large-sized waterbirds with long necks and legs, unwebbed feet and long, straight, dagger-shaped bills. The smaller, white herons are usually referred to as egrets. The sexes are alike in all species.

Lava Heron (adult)

SHOREBIRDS

In total, 34 species of shorebird have been recorded in Galápagos, only two of which are resident. The shorebirds can be conveniently divided into four groups, as shown in the following table. This shows the number of species recorded in each group and summarises their status. None of the species is endemic and only one is represented by an endemic subspecies.

Group (Plate No.)	Species Recorded	Status			Endemic Species	Endemic Subspecies
		Residents	Migrants	Vagrants		
Oystercatchers (18)	1	1				1
Stilts (18)	1	1				
Plovers (19)	6		2	4		
Sandpipers, phalaropes and allies (18, 20–24)	26		15	11		
Total:	34	2	17	15		1

OYSTERCATCHER
1 species recorded (resident)

Family: Haematopodidae
(Plate 18)

Endemic subspecies: American Oystercatcher

Oystercatchers are large shorebirds with medium-length legs and long, orange bills. The only species recorded in Galápagos, American Oystercatcher, has a distinctive black and white plumage. The sexes are alike.

American Oystercatcher (adult)

Black-necked Stilt (adults)

STILTS
Family: Recurvirostridae
1 species recorded (resident) **(Plate 18)**

Stilts are medium-sized shorebirds but are unmistakable due to their black and white plumage and exceptionally long legs. The sexes are similar.

Semipalmated Plover (adult, non-breeding)

PLOVERS
Family: Charadriidae
6 species recorded (2 migrants; 4 vagrants) **(Plate 19)**

Plovers are small to medium-sized, compact shorebirds with rather short necks; short, straight bills; and moderately long legs. They are readily told from other shorebirds by their behaviour, which involves periods of fast walking or running with sudden stops. The species recorded in Galápagos are from two distinct genera: the Charadrius plovers are small and characterised by the presence of breast-bands, whereas the Pluvialis plovers are medium-sized and show black bellies in breeding plumage (although in non-breeding plumage they are relatively uniform grey or brown).

Black-bellied Plover (juvenile)

SANDPIPERS, PHALAROPES and ALLIES
Family: Scolopacidae
26 species recorded (14 migrants; 12 vagrants) **(Plates 18 and 20–24)**

The other shorebirds recorded in Galápagos vary in size from the small sandpipers (often referred to as 'peeps') to the medium-sized Whimbrel. They also vary in structure from the short-legged to the long-legged and from the short-billed to the long-billed. The larger and strikingly plumaged species are generally quite easy to identify. However, the smaller ones can be difficult and some, particularly when they are in non-breeding plumage, are distinguishable only by careful observation of their overall structure, subtle plumage features, leg colour, bill shape and rump pattern.

Whimbrel (adult)

Wandering Tattler (adult)   *Red-necked Phalarope (juvenile)*

DIURNAL RAPTORS

Just three species of diurnal (or day-flying) raptor have been recorded in Galápagos, one of which is an endemic resident. Each of the species represents a different group, as shown in the following table:

Group (Plate No.)	Species Recorded	Residents	Migrants	Vagrants	Endemic Species	Endemic Subspecies
Osprey (25)	1		1			
Hawks (25)	1	1			1	
Falcons (25)	1		1			
Total:	3	1	2		1	

OSPREY   Family: Pandionidae
1 species recorded (migrant)   (Plate 25)

The Osprey is a large, broad-winged bird of prey with a hooked bill, powerful legs and feet, and sharp, curved talons. They feed exclusively on fish and have reversible outer toes and spiny foot pads which help them grasp their slippery prey. They are readily identified by their white underparts and dark upperparts. The sexes are alike and immature plumages resemble adult plumage.

Osprey (juvenile)

HAWKS   Family: Accipitridae
1 species recorded (resident)   (Plate 25)
Endemic species: GALÁPAGOS HAWK

Hawks are large, broad-winged birds of prey with hooked bills, a fleshy cere (the area at the base of the upper mandible), powerful legs and feet, and sharp, curved talons. The Galápagos Hawk is the only species to occur in Galápagos and is readily identified by its dark plumage. The sexes are alike although females are larger than males.

Galápagos Hawk (immature)

FALCONS   Family: Falconidae
1 species recorded (migrant)   (Plate 25)

Falcons are medium-sized birds of prey with long, pointed wings which are often held angled at the wrist or carpal joint, hooked bills, a fleshy cere, relatively short but powerful legs and feet, and sharp, curved talons. The sexes are alike although females are larger than males.

Peregrine (adult)

NIGHTBIRDS

Just three species of nightbird have been recorded in Galápagos, two of which are resident with endemic subspecies. Each of the species represents a different group, as shown in the following table:

Group (Plate No.)	Species Recorded	Status			Endemic Species	Endemic Subspecies
		Residents	Migrants	Vagrants		
Barn owls (26)	1	1				1
Typical owls (26)	1	1				1
Nightjars (26)	1			1		
Total:	3	2		1		2

Barn Owl (adult)

BARN OWLS
1 species recorded (resident)

Family: Tytonidae
(Plate 26)

Endemic subspecies: Barn Owl

Barn Owls are medium-sized, mainly nocturnal, birds of prey with long, broad, rather rounded wings; hooked bills; relatively long, slender legs; and sharp, curved talons. They are distinguished from other owls by their white, heart-shaped facial discs. The sexes are alike and immature plumages resemble adult plumage.

TYPICAL OWLS
1 species recorded (resident)

Family: Strigidae
(Plate 26)

Endemic subspecies: Short-eared Owl

The typical owls are small to large-sized, mainly nocturnal, birds of prey with long, broad, rounded wings; hooked bills; relatively short, powerful legs; and sharp, curved talons. The only species to occur in Galápagos, the Short-eared Owl, is medium-sized and readily told from the Barn Owl by its mainly dark plumage, dark, circular facial disc and yellow eyes. The sexes are alike and immature plumages resemble adult plumage.

Short-eared Owl (adult)

Common Nighthawk (adult male)

NIGHTJARS
1 species recorded (vagrant)

Family: Caprimulgidae
(Plate 26)

Nightjars are medium-sized, mostly nocturnal, birds with long, pointed wings which are held forward from the shoulder and crooked in flight. They have very short, thin bills but large gapes which enable them to catch moths and other insects in flight. Nightjars have very short legs and rest during the day on the ground or on branches where they are difficult to see due to their cryptic plumage. The only species recorded in Galápagos is the Common Nighthawk which shows white wing-flashes in flight. The sexes are similar and immature plumages resemble adult plumage.

LARGER LANDBIRDS

Eight species of larger landbird have been recorded in Galápagos, five of which are resident including one endemic species. The larger landbirds can be conveniently divided into three groups, as shown in the following table:

Group (Plate No.)	Species Recorded	Status			Endemic Species	Endemic Subspecies
		Residents	Migrants	Vagrants		
Pigeons/doves (27)	3	2			1	
Kingfishers (27)	1		1			
Cuckoos (28)	4	3		1		
Total:	8	5	1	2	1	

Galápagos Dove (adult)

PIGEONS AND DOVES
Family: Columbidae
(Plate 27)

3 species recorded (2 residents, including the introduced Feral Pigeon; 1 vagrant)

Endemic species: GALÁPAGOS DOVE

Pigeons and doves are small to medium-sized, rather plump birds with small heads which are bobbed back and forth when they are walking. They have relatively small, straight bills and short legs. In flight, pigeons and doves are fast and direct with rapid wingbeats. The sexes are alike and immature plumages resemble adult plumage.

Belted Kingfisher (adult female)

KINGFISHERS
Family: Alcedinidae
(Plate 27)

1 species recorded (migrant)

Kingfishers are small to medium-sized, stocky birds with short legs and necks, large heads and very large, dagger-shaped bills which are used to catch fish. The only species recorded in Galápagos, the Belted Kingfisher, is large with unmistakable plumage.

CUCKOOS
Family: Cuculidae
(Plate 28)

4 species recorded (3 residents; 1 vagrant)

Cuckoos are medium-sized, long-tailed, short-necked birds with long, pointed wings, resembling falcons in flight. They have short legs with two toes on each foot pointing forwards and two backwards. Most species of cuckoo have relatively short, stout bills, although the family also includes the black-plumaged anis which have large, ridged upper mandibles. Cuckoos are confined to the wetter, vegetated areas in Galápagos. The sexes are alike and immature plumages resemble adult plumage.

Dark-billed Cuckoo (adult)

AERIAL FEEDERS

Six species which feed exclusively on the wing (swifts, swallows and martins) have been recorded in Galápagos. Only one is resident, the endemic Galápagos Martin. The aerial feeders can conveniently be divided into two groups, as shown in the following table:

Group (Plate No.)	Species Recorded	Status			Endemic Species	Endemic Subspecies
		Residents	Migrants	Vagrants		
Swifts (29)	1			1		
Swallows and martins (29)	5	1	1	3	1	
Total:	**6**	**1**	**1**	**4**	**1**	

SWIFTS

Family: Apodidae
1 species recorded (vagrant) **(Plate 29)**

Swifts are small to medium-sized, fast-flying aerial feeders with cigar-shaped bodies and long, stiffly-held, sickle-shaped wings which bend close to the body. They do not perch since their feet are adapted to clinging on rock faces etc., all four toes pointing forward. Swifts have very short, thin bills but large gapes with which they catch insects in flight.

Chimney Swift

SWALLOWS and MARTINS

Family: Hirundinidae
5 species recorded (1 resident; 1 migrant; 3 vagrants) **(Plate 29)**

Endemic species: GALÁPAGOS MARTIN

Swallows and martins are small, aerial feeders with rather slender bodies and long, pointed wings which are held angled in flight, the wrist or carpal joint being further from the body than in swifts. They are extremely manœuverable and their short, pointed bills and wide gapes are well adapted for catching their invertebrate food in the air. Swallows and martins have very short legs but are able to perch.

Galápagos Martin
(adult male)

SMALLER LANDBIRDS

In total, 29 species of smaller landbird have been recorded in Galápagos, 20 of which are resident. Eighteen of these resident species are endemic to Galápagos and the other two are represented by endemic subspecies. The smaller landbirds can be conveniently divided into ten groups, as shown in the following table:

Type (Plate No.)	Species Recorded	Status			Endemic Species	Endemic Subspecies
		Residents	Migrants	Vagrants		
Flycatchers (30)	3	2		1	1	1
New World warblers (31)	2	1		1		1
Vireos (31)	1			1		
Bananaquit (31)	1			1		
Waxwings (32)	1			1		
Grosbeaks (32)	2			2		
Tanagers (32)	1			1		
New World blackbirds (32)	1			1		
Mockingbirds (33)	4	4			4	
Darwin's finches (34–37)	13	13			13	
Total:	**29**	**20**		**9**	**18**	**2**

TYRANT FLYCATCHERS
Family: Tyrannidae
3 species recorded (2 residents; 1 vagrant) **(Plate 30)**

Endemic species: LARGE-BILLED (OR GALÁPAGOS) FLYCATCHER

Endemic subspecies: Vermilion Flycatcher

Vermilion Flycatcher (adult male)

Flycatchers are small birds with large heads; short, broad-based, flat bills; and short legs. They have a rather erect posture and feed by making sallies from exposed perches to catch passing insects. The two species resident in Galápagos are readily identifiable.

NEW WORLD WARBLERS
Family: Parulidae
2 species recorded (1 resident; 1 vagrant) **(Plate 31)**

Endemic subspecies: Yellow Warbler

New World warblers are small birds with short, thin, pointed bills. They inhabit vegetated areas and are generally very active, feeding by picking insects from the leaves or branches. The only resident species in Galápagos, the Yellow Warbler, is readily identified.

Yellow Warbler (adult male)

VIREOS
Family: Vireonidae
1 species recorded (vagrant) **(Plate 31)**

Vireos are small perching birds, reminiscent of warblers but rather more chunky with heavier bills. They are less active than warblers and the only species recorded in Galápagos, the Red-eyed Vireo, has a distinctive head pattern.

Red-eyed Vireo (adult)

BANANAQUIT
Family: Coerebidae
1 species recorded (vagrant) **(Plate 31)**

The Bananaquit is a small, warbler-like bird with a relatively long, thin, decurved bill. The plumage is distinctive with yellow underparts, dark upperparts and (in the adult) black and white head pattern.

Bananaquit (adult)

WAXWINGS
Family: Bombycillidae
1 species recorded (vagrant) **(Plate 32)**

Waxwings are medium-sized, rather plump perching birds with prominent, sleek crests; short, broad-based bills; short legs; pointed wings; and relatively short tails. Their plumage is rather sombre although they have characteristic yellow-tipped tails and red waxy tips to their secondary feathers.

Cedar Waxwing (adult)

GROSBEAKS
Family: Emberizidae
2 species recorded (both vagrants) **(Plate 32)**

Grosbeaks are small to medium-sized, rather stocky perching birds with short, heavy bills; longish tails; and relatively short, broad wings. Although males of the two species recorded in Galápagos are readily identifiable in breeding plumage, females and immatures are less distinctive.

Rose-breasted Grosbeak (adult female)

TANAGERS

Summer Tanager (adult female)

Family: Emberizidae
Subfamily: Thraupinae
1 species recorded (vagrant)   **(Plate 32)**

Tanagers are medium-sized, fairly robust perching birds with toothed, conical bills. Adult males are generally brightly coloured and easily identified. Females and immatures of the only species recorded in Galápagos, the Summer Tanager, are rather dowdy.

NEW WORLD BLACKBIRDS

1 species recorded (vagrant)

Family: Aceridae
(Plate 32)

The only species of New World blackbird recorded in Galápagos is the Bobolink. This species is medium-sized with a longish, rather ragged-tipped tail and short, conical bill. Males are readily identified in breeding plumage but females and juveniles are brown and streaked.

Bobolink (juvenile)

MOCKINGBIRDS

Galápagos Mockingbird (adult)

Family: Mimidae
4 species recorded (all resident)   **(Plate 33)**

Endemic species: GALÁPAGOS MOCKINGBIRD; CHARLES (OR FLOREANA) MOCKINGBIRD; HOOD MOCKINGBIRD; CHATHAM (OR SAN CRISTÓBAL) MOCKINGBIRD

Mockingbirds are medium-sized landbirds with long tails, longish legs and long, narrow, decurved bills. The plumage of the species in Galápagos is rather drab, with brownish upperparts and pale underparts.

DARWIN'S FINCHES

13 species recorded (all resident)

Family: Emberizidae
Subfamily: Emberizinae
(Plates 34–37)

Endemic species: SHARP-BEAKED GROUND FINCH; LARGE GROUND FINCH; MEDIUM GROUND FINCH; SMALL GROUND FINCH; LARGE TREE FINCH; MEDIUM TREE FINCH; SMALL TREE FINCH; VEGETARIAN FINCH; CACTUS FINCH; LARGE CACTUS FINCH; WOODPECKER FINCH; MANGROVE FINCH; WARBLER FINCH

Small Ground Finch (adult male)

Darwin's (or Galápagos) Finches are small landbirds with generally dull black, brown or olive, often streaky, plumage; short tails; and short, rounded wings. Their bills vary greatly in size and shape (a fact which was instrumental in inspiring Charles Darwin's thinking in relation to the theory of evolution - and hence the name given to this fascinating group of species). Darwin's Finches are found in all the habitats on Galápagos. Identification can be notoriously difficult due to the variation within each species and the occurrence of hybrids. For this reason, not all birds can be confidently identified to specific level and confusing individuals are probably best ignored!

Warbler Finch (adult)

The bird plates

Species order The order in which the species appear on the plates in this book does not follow precisely the taxonomic sequence adopted in most bird books. For ease of reference, the plates have instead been ordered so that all the birds of one 'type' (e.g. the seabirds) are together. Similarly, the species which are most likely to be confused appear, as far as possible, on the same plate. The text follows the sequence in which the species appear on the plate, from top to bottom. The species are numbered sequentially and the following annotations

1	Adult in breeding plumage (species 1)
1n	Adult in non-breeding plumage
1m Male	**1f** Female
1f-w First-winter	**1s-w** Second-winter
1i Immature	**1j** Juvenile
1c Chick	

Distribution maps A distribution map accompanies the text for each of the resident species. To save space, three 'groups' of islands have been moved: the islands of Darwin and Wolf being shown in a small square at the top left of the map; Pinta, Marchena and Genovesa in the rectangle at the top right of the map; and San Cristóbal and Española in the rectangle to the bottom right. The true position of each of the islands is shown on the map which appears on the front endpaper of the book; this map also gives the

names of each of the islands. A key to the colour codes used on the maps is shown on this 'dummy' map.

- ▨ Breeding range
- ▨ Non-beeding range
- • Breeding colony
- ◥ Nesting area
- ▨ Regularly seen at sea
- ▨ Occasionally seen at sea
- ▨ Rarely seen at sea

English name The English names used in the book are those most commonly used in recent literature. Alternative names which are also used regularly are shown in brackets.

Spanish name The Spanish names shown are those which are most regularly used in Galápagos.

Endemic species and subspecies The names of species which are endemic to Galápagos are preceded by an **E** and those which are represented by endemic subspecies by an **e**.

Status The first part of the text for each species provides information on its status. This includes details of whether it is a resident, migrant or vagrant. For residents and migrants, a subjective assessment of abundance is given (and, where known, population estimates are shown). Endemic subspecies are named where appropriate and, for resident species, a summary of their breeding season(s) and habitat preferences is included.

Conservation status An indication of the conservation status of species which are threatened with extinction is given at the end of the first paragraph. The categories used are explained in the introduction to the birds on page 17, and are shown in **Red Type**.

Measurements The length of a bird is the measurement taken from the tip of the bill to the tip of the tail, with the bird lying flat on its back. For species which are regularly seen in flight a wingspan measurement is also included; this is the distance from wing-tip to wing-tip with the wings extended. Details of measurements are included in this book principally to give an indication of the relative size of each species.

Identification Details of the features which are key to the identification of the species are given, with brief descriptions of the different plumages where appropriate. Distinctions are made between male and female, breeding and non-breeding, and adult, immature and juvenile plumages where necessary. Where no such distinction is made, it should be assumed that the plumages are similar.

Voice The voices of birds are often difficult to describe since the perception of a call or song varies greatly from one person to another. However, where it is helpful to the identification of the species, details of relevant calls or songs are given.

Behaviour Particular behavioural characteristics which help in the identification of a species, such as the flight action of seabirds, are highlighted where appropriate.

PLATE 1

e **1** **Brown Pelican** *Pelecanus occidentalis* Pelicano Café

| Length: 105–152 cm |
| Wingspan: 203–228 cm |

Common resident; endemic subspecies *urinator*. Population estimated at a few thousand pairs; breeds throughout the year, nesting in small colonies in low bushes and mangroves, occasionally on the ground.

IDENTIFICATION: Unmistakable, due to very large size and long, characteristic bill. Adult: Sexes alike, although females generally slightly smaller than males. Plumage mainly grey-brown, with chestnut and white markings on head and neck. Immature: Resembles adult but lacks head and neck markings and has pale underparts.

VOICE: Adults usually silent; young birds on the nest hiss and clap bill.

BEHAVIOUR: Often feeds by plunge-diving from the air, usually close inshore. Accomplished fliers, regularly seen soaring on thermals. Often fly to or from feeding grounds in orderly rows, with birds flapping and gliding almost in unison.

E **2** **Flightless (or Galápagos) Cormorant** *Phalacrocorax harrisi*

Cormorán no Volador

| Length: 89–100 cm |

Uncommon, localised resident. Population estimated at *c.* 700–800 pairs in c. 100 small colonies, but declines dramatically after El Niño years. Nests on sheltered rocky shores, building bulky nest predominantly of seaweed just above the high-water mark. Breeds throughout the year, although most eggs are laid from March to September. Conservation Status: **Vulnerable**.

IDENTIFICATION: Unmistakable; the only cormorant in Galápagos, with apparently functionless 'tatty' wings. Adult: Sexes alike, although males noticeably larger than females; plumage dark blackish-brown above, paler brown below; eyes turquoise. Immature: Resembles adult but has glossy-black plumage and dull brown eyes.

VOICE: Adults give a low growl; young birds on the nest give a plaintive *"wee-wee…"*.

BEHAVIOUR: Flightless and marine; feeds by diving, usually close inshore.

E **3** **Galápagos Penguin** *Spheniscus mendiculus* Pingüino de las Galápagos

| Length: 48–52 cm |

Uncommon, localised resident. Population fluctuates between a few thousand and a few hundred birds, declining dramatically after El Niño years. Nests in loose colonies in burrows or crevices close to the shore, breeding throughout the year depending on food availability. Conservation Status: **Vulnerable**.

IDENTIFICATION: Unmistakable; the only penguin in Galápagos. Adult: Sexes alike, although males are slightly larger than females. Upperparts, flippers and face black (brown when worn), with white line running through the eyes, down cheeks and across throat; underparts white with black line across breast and down flanks. Immature: Resembles adult but greyer and lacks the head and chest pattern.

VOICE: A braying sound reminiscent of a donkey.

BEHAVIOUR: Flightless and pelagic, diving to feed.

PLATE 2

❶ Black-browed Albatross   *Diomedea melanophris*   Albatros de Ceja Negra

Length: 83–93 cm
Wingspan: *c.* 240 cm

Vagrant; one record.

IDENTIFICATION: Size and shape as Waved Albatross, from which distinguished by diagnostic combination of black upperwing, back and tail, and white head and body with dark smudge through eye. ADULT: Underwing mainly dark with variable width white stripe; bill orange-yellow. IMMATURE: As adult but underwing and bill darker.

❷ Southern Giant Petrel   *Macronectes giganteus*   Petrel Gigante Común

Length: 86–99 cm
Wingspan: 185–205 cm

Vagrant; one record.

IDENTIFICATION: Large albatross-sized petrel, told from Waved Albatross by uniform grey-brown plumage with whitish face and breast (less obvious in juveniles) and silvery-grey underwing. At close range, prominent 'tube-nose' and yellow eye diagnostic. Has a distinctive hump-backed appearance in flight.

❸ Wandering Albatross   *Diomedea exulans*   Albatros Paseador
❹ Royal Albatross   *Diomedea epomophora*   Albatros Real

Length: 107–122 cm/
107–135 cm

Wingspan: 254–351 cm/
305–351 cm

Vagrant; two records, not specifically identified. Conservation Status of Wandering Albatross: VULNERABLE.

IDENTIFICATION: Extremely large albatrosses. The two species are separated with difficulty (see e.g. Harrison 1983). Wandering follows ships; Royal does not. ADULTS AND SUBADULTS (BOTH SPECIES) AND JUVENILE ROYAL: Distinguished from other albatrosses by diagnostic combination of wholly white head, body and back, and black upperwing with at least some white markings in centre or along leading edge. Underwing white with narrow black trailing-edge. At close range dark cutting edge to mandibles is diagnostic of Royal. JUVENILE WANDERING: Unique combination of brown body and upperwings, and white face.

❺ Black-footed Albatross   *Diomedea nigripes*   Albatros de Piés Negros

Length: 68–74 cm
Wingspan: 193–213 cm

Vagrant; one confirmed record in the waters between Galápagos and the mainland; possible record from Española in 1897.

IDENTIFICATION: A small albatross, distinguished from Waved Albatross by diagnostic wholly dark brown plumage with white areas at base of bill, on uppertail-coverts (adults only) and often on undertail-coverts.

Ⓔ ❻ Waved Albatross   *Diomedea irrorata*   Albatros

Length: 85–93 cm
Wingspan: 230–240 cm

Localised resident, breeding only on Española. Total population estimated at c. 50,000–70,000 birds, including at least 18,200 breeding pairs. Breeds from March to January, nesting on the ground. Conservation Status: NEAR-THREATENED.

IDENTIFICATION: Unmistakable; due to large size and very long wings; the largest breeding bird in Galápagos. ADULT: Sexes alike, although males are generally slightly larger than females. Plumage mainly grey-brown with pale head and neck, and back of neck tinged yellow; underwings white with dark trailing-edge. Bill large and yellow. IMMATURE: Resembles adult but head whiter and bill dull.

VOICE: Silent at sea but gives a long, loud "*whoo–oo*" during display.

BEHAVIOUR: Pelagic. Very accomplished fliers, gliding for prolonged periods without flapping, particularly in windy conditions. Feeds from the surface, usually far out to sea. Performs bill-snapping and bill-rattling courtship display at breeding colony, mainly towards the end of the breeding season.

PLATE 3

❶ Parkinson's Black Petrel *Procellaria parkinsoni*   Petrel de Parkinson

Length: 46 cm
Wingspan: 115 cm

Vagrant; 3 specimens collected during an expedition in 1905 are the only records. Conservation Status: **VULNERABLE**.

IDENTIFICATION: A large, heavily-built petrel with buoyant flight on slightly bowed wings. Plumage entirely blackish-brown except for pale shafts to primaries on underwings. Combination of pale bill with dark tip and black feet is diagnostic.

❷ Pink-footed Shearwater *Puffinus creatopus*   Pardela Negruzca

Length: 48 cm
Wingspan: 109 cm

Vagrant; recorded at sea off Isabela and Pinzón from October to January. Conservation Status: **VULNERABLE**.

IDENTIFICATION: A large, heavily-built shearwater which flies in a rather 'lumbering' manner, with straight wings usually held forward. Plumage variable but generally greyish-brown upperparts, pale underparts, and palish mottled underwings with ill-defined dark trailing-edge and tips. Combination of flesh-pink bill with dark tip and pink feet is diagnostic.

❸ Sooty Shearwater *Puffinus griseus*   Pufino Negro

Length: 40–51 cm
Wingspan: 94–109 cm

Regular visitor in small numbers.

IDENTIFICATION: A large, stockily-built shearwater which usually flies fast with rather stiff wings; often 'towers' in strong winds. Plumage wholly dark except for diagnostic silvery underwings. Bill dark.

❹ Wedge-tailed Shearwater *Puffinus pacificus*   Pardela del Pacífico

Length: 38–46 cm
Wingspan: 97–105 cm

Vagrant; one record of a bird found predated by a Short-eared Owl on Plazas. Occurs commonly in waters to the north of Galápagos so possibly overlooked.

IDENTIFICATION: A large, long-winged shearwater which flies in a characteristic buoyant, drifting manner with wings held bowed and well forward. Tail long and pointed. Occurs in two colour morphs, dark and pale. The pale morph is most likely to occur and has brown upperparts and crown, white underparts and white underwings with well-defined dark trailing-edge and wing-tip. Bill uniform, grey to pink.

❺ ❺ Galápagos Shearwater *Puffinus subalaris*   Pufino

Length: 27–33 cm
Wingspan: 64–74 cm

Common resident; formerly considered to be an endemic subspecies of Audubon's Shearwater *Puffinus lherminieri* but recent studies have shown that it should be treated as a full species. Population estimated at c. 10,000 pairs in about *c*. 30 colonies; breeds throughout the year, nesting in crevices or burrows which are visited during the day.

IDENTIFICATION: A small shearwater; the only species breeding in Galápagos. Blackish upperparts and crown, white underparts and throat. Underwings white with dark trailing-edge and wing-tip.

VOICE: Usually silent at sea, but a loud "*kee–kaa–cooo*" is given near the breeding colony.

BEHAVIOUR: Pelagic. Flight direct, often just skimming the surface of the sea, with stiff wings and rapid wingbeats interspersed with short glides. Often forms large feeding flocks, sometimes close inshore. Feeds by plunge-diving from or close to the surface.

PLATE 4

1 **Cape Petrel**   *Daption capense*   Petrel de Cabo

Length: 38–40 cm
Wingspan: 81–91 cm

Vagrant; one record in Galápagos waters. Regularly seen in waters between the archipelago and the mainland.

IDENTIFICATION: A medium-sized petrel. Distinctive, although variable, pattern of dark brown and white blotching on upperwing; underparts white with some dark spotting, but head dark.

2 **Southern Fulmar**   *Fulmarus glacialoides*   Petrel Plateado

Length: 46–50 cm
Wingspan: 114–120 cm

Vagrant; one record.

IDENTIFICATION: A medium-sized, rather stockily-built petrel with characteristic gliding flight on stiff but slightly bowed wings. Upperwing, back and tail pale blue-grey with contrasting dark trailing-edge to wing, and dark outer-wing with variable pale patch at base of inner primaries; underparts white.

3 **Mottled Petrel**   *Pterodroma inexpectata*   Petrel Moteado

Length: 33–35 cm
Wingspan: 74–82 cm

Vagrant; recorded at sea off Galápagos.

IDENTIFICATION: A medium-sized, long-winged petrel rarely seen close to land. Characteristic flight action involves high, bounding arcs. Distinguished from similar Dark-rumped Petrel by black 'W' shape across the upperwings; grey head, neck and rump; broad black line across underwings; and dark grey belly contrasting with white undertail-coverts.

4 **Antarctic Prion**   *Pachyptila desolata*   Petrel Ballena

Length: 25–30 cm
Wingspan: 56–66 cm

Vagrant; only record is of a bird found dead on Floreana.

IDENTIFICATION: A small, blue-grey petrel with distinctive black 'M' mark across upperwing and dark tip to tail. Underparts white with dark mottling on sides of breast forming a partial collar. Underside of tail white with dark tip and central line. At close range dark 'mask' through eye and white mark above eye visible.

5 **Gould's (or White-winged) Petrel**   *Pterodroma leucoptera*   Petrel de Gould

Length: 30 cm
Wingspan: 70–71 cm

Vagrant; recorded at sea off Galápagos.

IDENTIFICATION: A medium-sized, long-winged petrel rarely seen close to land. Characteristic flight action, at times reminiscent of Audubon's Shearwater, with a series of rapid wingbeats followed by a low, stiff-winged glide, but has sudden turns of speed involving jinking and banking in steep arcs before returning to flap–glide flight action. Distinguished from similar Dark-rumped Petrel by black 'W' shape across the upperwings, sooty-black crown and hindneck forming a distinct hood, and dark-tipped grey tail.

e **6** **Dark-rumped Petrel**   *Pterodroma phaeopygia*   Patapegada

Length: 43 cm
Wingspan: 91 cm

Uncommon resident; endemic subspecies *phaeopygia* often treated as a separate species: 'Galápagos Petrel'. Population estimated at 10,000–50,000 pairs in four colonies located in the highlands; breeds throughout the year, with different colonies nesting at different times; nests in burrows which are visited only at night. Conservation Status: **CRITICALLY ENDANGERED**.

IDENTIFICATION: A large, long-winged petrel. Upperparts, crown and side of neck and breast uniform brownish-black; underparts and sides of rump white; conspicuous white forehead; underwing white with black line running along forewing and across centre of wing towards body. Small black mark in 'armpits' diagnostic.

VOICE: Silent at sea but calls at night near breeding colony "*kee–kee–kee— (c)ooo*".

BEHAVIOUR: Pelagic. Flight action characteristic: in calm weather involving a series of 3 or 4 flaps followed by a long glide on bowed and angled wings; in windy conditions glides in spectacular long arcs, high above the water, with wings bowed. Usually found well away from land during the day. Feeds from the surface whilst resting on the sea or by dipping in flight.

PLATE 5

ⓔ ➊ Wedge-rumped Storm-petrel *Oceanodroma tethys*

Golondrina de Tormenta de Galapágos

Length: 18–20 cm
Wingspan: *c.* 50 cm

Common resident; endemic subspecies *tethys*. Population estimated at *c.* 200,000 pairs in 3 colonies. Nests colonially in burrows or crevices, breeding throughout the year but mainly during the cold season (April to October). Conservation Status: **Near-threatened**.

IDENTIFICATION: A medium-sized, relatively long, narrow-winged storm-petrel. Upperparts uniform dark brown with paler brown bar on upperwing and large, triangular-shaped, pure white rump which extends almost to the tip of the tail and to the upper flanks and lateral undertail-coverts. Underparts dark, sometimes with ill-defined pale centre to underwings.

BEHAVIOUR: Pelagic. Flight fast and rather forceful with deep wingbeats and involving much banking and twisting, often high over the waves. Typically flies with wings held bowed and angled slightly forwards. When feeding skips and bounds over the surface, sometimes pattering on the water in a manner reminiscent of Elliot's Storm-petrel. Unique among storm-petrels in visiting the breeding grounds by day and feeding at night. Occasionally follows ships.

➋ Madeiran (or Band-rumped) Storm-petrel *Oceanodroma castro*

Golondrina de Madeira

Length: 19–21 cm
Wingspan: 44–46 cm

Uncommon resident. Population estimated at *c.* 15,000 pairs in *c.* 15 colonies. Nests in burrows or crevices, breeding throughout the year, with two different populations nesting in the same areas at different times.

IDENTIFICATION: A medium-sized storm-petrel with relatively broad, blunt-tipped wings; moderately long, slightly forked tail; and a rather 'bull-necked' appearance. The legs do not protrude beyond tail in flight. Upperparts uniform dark brown with paler brown bar on upperwing. Narrow, but prominent, 'U'-shaped white rump extends to the lateral undertail-coverts; at close range may show dark feathers at rear of white rump. Underparts entirely dark.

VOICE: Silent at sea but calls at night near the breeding colony: a squeaky "*whikka–whikka…*" rather like rubbing a wet finger on a glass.

BEHAVIOUR: Pelagic, feeding well offshore and rarely seen close to land. Flight action rather buoyant with rapid, shallow wingbeats and low, shearing glides reminiscent of Audubon's Shearwater, with the wings held flat or slightly bowed. Progresses in a zigzag manner but occasionally becomes erratic, banking and 'jinking' and doubling back. Does not follow ships but sometimes attracted to lights at night. Visits colonies nocturnally.

ⓔ ➌ Elliot's (or White-vented) Storm-petrel *Oceanites gracilis*

Golondrina de Tormenta de Elliot

Length: 15–16 cm
Wingspan: 40 cm

Common resident; endemic subspecies *galapagoensis*. Population estimated at many thousands and although a nest has yet to be found in Galápagos, breeding is suspected to occur between April and October. Conservation Status: **Data Deficient**.

IDENTIFICATION: A small storm-petrel with relatively short, broad-based and rather rounded wings, and a square-ended tail with feet protruding beyond tail in flight. Upperparts uniform dark brown with paler brown bar on upperwings and a narrow but prominent, 'U'-shaped, pure white rump which extends to the rear flanks. Underparts dark with pale grey patch on centre of belly, and ill-defined pale bar on underwings.

BEHAVIOUR: Pelagic, although often feeds close to shore. Feeds in a distinctive manner, fluttering and pattering on the water with wings raised. Often follows ships.

PLATE 6

❶ White-bellied Storm-petrel   *Fregetta grallaria*   Bailarín

Length: 19–20 cm
Wingspan: 46 cm

Vagrant; few records, mainly at sea to the south of Galápagos from May to August.

IDENTIFICATION: A medium-sized storm-petrel with rather broad, rounded wings and long legs which project just beyond tail. Characteristic direct flight, very close to the water surface with legs dangling and body swinging from side to side, often plunging breast-first into the water and then springing clear. Upperparts dark brown with prominent pale bar on upperwing contrasting with black flight feathers. Prominent, broad 'U'-shaped white rump extending to white breast and belly. Head and upper breast dark brown. Underwing coverts white, contrasting with dark flight feathers and leading edge of wing. Occasionally follows ships.

❷ White-faced Storm-petrel   *Pelagodroma marina*   Golondrina Cariblanca

Length: 20–21 cm
Wingspan: 41–43 cm

Vagrant; three records.

IDENTIFICATION: A medium-sized storm-petrel with broad, rather rounded wings, and feet projecting well beyond tail in flight. Flight action rather erratic, involving much banking and weaving often with jerky and rhythmic wingbeats somewhat reminiscent of Spotted Sandpiper. When feeding, 'dances' along the water surface with body swinging from side to side, the long legs being lowered only at the last minute before touching the surface. Upperparts grey-brown with pale bar on upperwing contrasting with black flight feathers; rump pale grey contrasting with black tail. Underparts and underwing-coverts white, contrasting with dark flight feathers. Brown and white face pattern distinctive. Rarely follows ships.

❸ Leach's Storm-petrel   *Oceanodroma leucorhoa*   Golondrina de Mar

Length: 19–22 cm
Wingspan: 45–48 cm

Vagrant; few records but possibly overlooked due to similarity with other species.

IDENTIFICATION: A largish storm-petrel with relatively long, narrow wings which are usually held bowed and slightly forward. Flight buoyant and rather bounding with deep, tern-like wingbeats and low, shearing glides. Tail longish and forked, although fork not always visible. Upperparts dark brown with prominent pale brown bar on upperwing contrasting with dark flight feathers. Narrow, 'V'-shaped white rump with dark line up the centre (can be difficult to see). (Beware that dark-rumped birds may also occur and could be confused with Markham's or Black Storm-petrels.) Underparts wholly dark.

❹ Black Storm-petrel   *Oceanodroma melania*   Golondrina de Tormenta Negra

Length: 23 cm
Wingspan: 46–51 cm

Vagrant; two records but possibly overlooked due to confusion particularly with Markham's Storm-petrel. A warm-water species and therefore most likely to occur in El Niño years.

IDENTIFICATION: A largish, 'dark-rumped' storm-petrel with relatively long wings. Flight buoyant and rather direct, with deep wingbeats reminiscent of Black Tern (the wings being raised and lowered to c.60° above and below the horizontal) and occasional glides. Tail noticeably forked (although less deeply than Markham's). Upperparts dark brownish-black with prominent pale bar on upperwing not reaching the leading edge. Confusion likely only with Markham's and dark-rumped Leach's Storm-petrels, from which best separated on flight action. Occasionally follows ships.

❺ Markham's Storm-petrel   *Oceanodroma markhami*   Golondrina de Markham

Length: 23 cm
Wingspan: c. 50 cm

Vagrant; occasional records.

IDENTIFICATION: A largish, 'dark-rumped' storm-petrel with relatively long wings. Flight buoyant, with deliberate, shallow wingbeats (rarely more than 30° above and below the horizontal) and regular glides. Tail deeply and noticeably forked. Upperparts dark brown with prominent pale bar on upperwing reaching the leading edge and contrasting with dark flight feathers. Confusion likely only with Black and dark-rumped Leach's Storm-petrels, from which best separated on flight action. Does not normally follow ships.

PLATE 7

e **1** **Magnificent Frigatebird** *Fregata magnificens* Fragata Real

Length: 89–114 cm
Wingspan: 217–214 cm

Resident, endemic subspecies *magnificens*. Population estimated at *c*. 1,000 pairs in 12 colonies; breeds throughout the year.

IDENTIFICATION: A large, dark, long-winged seabird with rakish flight and long, deeply forked tail. Slightly larger than very similar Great Frigatebird which is the only likely confusion species. ADULT MALE: Wholly black (apart from red gular sac); purplish sheen to mantle feathers, and black or brown legs and feet diagnostic. In flight very difficult to distinguish from Great Frigatebird, although usually lacks the pale bar across the upperwing which is typical of Great. ADULT FEMALE: Similar to male but breast white. Blue eye-ring diagnostic. In flight very similar to Great Frigatebird but white breast and black throat and thin white lines on axillaries are diagnostic. JUVENILE: Resembles female but head as well as breast white.

Note that since birds do not reach maturity until their fourth year, gradually developing adult plumage during this period, a series of intermediate plumages occur, often making specific identification difficult. Immature birds do, however, often show some thin white lines on the axillaries.

VOICE: Silent at sea, but male makes a drawn-out "*oo–oo–oo–...*" sound when displaying at the breeding colony.

BEHAVIOUR: Generally feeds close inshore, mainly by kleptoparasitising passing seabirds, particularly Blue-footed Boobies. When displaying, males inflate their bright red gular sac like a balloon and call to attract females, at the same time vibrating their outstretched wings.

2 **Great Frigatebird** *Fregata minor* Fragata Común

Length: 86–100 cm
Wingspan: 203–230 cm

Resident. Population estimated at a few thousand pairs in 12 colonies; breeds throughout the year.

IDENTIFICATION: A large, dark, long-winged seabird with rakish flight and long, deeply forked tail. Slightly smaller than very similar Magnificent Frigatebird which is the only likely confusion species. ADULT MALE: Wholly black (apart from red gular sac); green sheen to mantle feathers, and red or reddish-brown legs and feet diagnostic. In flight very difficult to distinguish from Magnificent, although usually shows a pale bar across upperwing. ADULT FEMALE: Similar to male but breast and throat white. Red or pink eye-ring diagnostic. In flight very similar to Magnificent Frigatebird but throat white and does not show white markings on axillaries. JUVENILE: Resembles female but head and breast usually washed pale orange or tawny is diagnostic. However, white-headed juveniles sometimes occur and are inseparable from juvenile Magnificent.

Note that since birds do not reach maturity until their fourth year, gradually developing adult plumage during this period, a series of intermediate plumages occur, making separation from Magnificent Frigatebird all the more difficult.

VOICE: Silent at sea but male gives a continuous rattling call when displaying at the breeding colony.

BEHAVIOUR: A rather more pelagic species than Magnificent Frigatebird, generally only being seen near land in the vicinity of the breeding colonies (which tend to be on the outer islands of Galápagos). Feeds mainly by picking food from the surface although, like Magnificent, regularly kleptoparasitises other seabirds. When displaying, males inflate their bright red gular sac like a balloon and call to attract females, at the same time vibrating their outstretched wings.

PLATE 8

❶ Red-footed Booby *Sula sula* Piquero Patas Rojas

Length: 66–77 cm
Wingspan: 91–101 cm

Common but rather localised resident. Population estimated at *c.* 250,000 pairs (including *c.* 140,000 pairs on Genovesa). Breeds throughout the year, nesting colonially in trees (the other boobies nest on the ground).

IDENTIFICATION: ADULT: Two colour forms: brown ⬤1bf and white ⬤1wf (c.95% of Galápagos population is of the brown form); both forms have diagnostic combination of red feet and blue bill. JUVENILE: Resembles brown form of adult but feet dark; distinguished from other juvenile boobies by wholly brown underparts.

BEHAVIOUR: Courtship display, performed on branches near nest, involves birds lifting their feet and waving them in the air. Partially nocturnal, feeding well away from land. This perhaps explains why it is less frequently encountered at sea than other boobies despite being the most numerous species in Galápagos.

❷ Nazca Booby *Sula granti* Piquero Enmascarado; Piquero Blanco

Length: 81–92 cm
Wingspan: *c.* 152 cm

Common resident. Population *c.* 25,000–50,000 pairs. Breeds throughout the year, with colonies on different islands nesting at different times (e.g. eggs laid on Genovesa between August and November and on Española between November and February); nests on the ground. Formerly treated as a subspecies of Masked Booby *Sula dactylatra* but now afforded full species status.

IDENTIFICATION: ADULT: Sexes alike, although females usually slightly larger with duller bill; only black and white booby with orange-yellow bill. JUVENILE: White underparts with distinct brown 'bib', the white breast extending to form a narrow white collar.

BEHAVIOUR: Usually feeds well away from land.

e ❸ Blue-footed Booby *Sula nebouxii* Piquero Patas Azules

Length: 76–84 cm
Wingspan: *c.* 152 cm

Common resident; endemic subspecies *excisa*. Population estimated at c. 10,000 pairs; breeds throughout the year, nesting on the ground.

IDENTIFICATION: ADULT: Sexes alike, although females have pigmented area around iris making pupil appear larger; blue feet diagnostic. JUVENILE: Resembles juvenile Nazca Booby but lacks well-defined brown 'bib' of that species and shows white patch at base of hindneck and white rump.

VOICE: At breeding colony, males give a plaintive whistle whereas females and immatures give a hoarse "*quack*".

BEHAVIOUR: Courtship display, performed near nest, involves birds lifting their feet and waving them in the air. Usually feeds close inshore.

❹ Brown Booby *Sula leucogaster* Piquero Pardo

Length: 64–74 cm
Wingspan: 132–150 cm

Vagrant; one confirmed record of an adult. Occurs regularly in waters to the north of Galápagos so possibly overlooked.

IDENTIFICATION: ADULT: Most likely to be confused with juvenile Nazca Booby, from which distinguished in flight by yellow bill and lack of white collar. JUVENILE: Resembles adult, but duller with underparts mottled brown.

PLATE 9

ⓔ ① Swallow-tailed Gull   *Creagrus furcatus*   Gaviota de Cola Bifurcada

Length: 51–58 cm
Wingspan: *c.* 130 cm

Common resident, especially in the easternmost islands. Population c. 10,000–15,000 pairs in over 50 colonies. Endemic, except for a small colony on Malpelo Island off the west coast of Colombia. Breeds throughout the year, nesting in the shore zone.

IDENTIFICATION: Unmistakable; the only common whitish gull with a distinctive forked tail. ADULT: Upperparts and neck grey; underparts white. In breeding plumage has dark grey head, large eye with red eye-ring, and black bill with pale base and tip. Non-breeding adults have white head with dark eye-patch. In flight shows distinctive 'triangular' pattern of grey back and wing-coverts, white secondaries and black primaries. JUVENILE: Head and underparts white, with black eye-patch and ear-spot; upperparts scaly brown and white.

VOICE: Gives a range of calls which may have a function in echolocation; most frequent alarm call is a rattle interspersed with a piercing "*pee*".

BEHAVIOUR: Feeds mostly nocturnally, usually several miles from land. Flight buoyant and tern-like.

ⓔ ② Lava Gull   *Larus fuliginosus*   Gavioto de Lava

Length: 51–55 cm
Wingspan: *c.* 130 cm

Widely distributed resident. The total world population occurs on Galápagos and is fewer than 400 pairs. Conservation status: **VULNERABLE**. Breeds throughout the year, but mainly from May to October, nesting singly in the shore zone.

IDENTIFICATION: Unmistakable; the only all-dark gull, with heavy bill. ADULT: Blackish head with white eyelids, sooty-grey upperparts and breast, paler on belly. In flight, darker primaries contrast with rest of wing; rump and outer tail feathers whitish. JUVENILE: Dark chocolate-brown overall, except for pale rump. FIRST-WINTER/FIRST-SUMMER: Similar to juvenile, but has greyer tints to head and upperparts.

BEHAVIOUR: A tideline scavenger, rarely alighting on the sea.

③ Pomarine Jaeger/Skua   *Stercorarius pomarinus*   Salteador

Length: 46–51 cm
Wingspan: 125–138 cm

Vagrant; few records, but probably overlooked as the waters off western South America are one of its main non-breeding ranges.

IDENTIFICATION: A smaller, slimmer version of South Polar Skua with distinctive broad tail-streamers, although these are lacking in juveniles and some adults. Wings show pale flashes at base of primaries. ADULT: Occurs in two colour phases: pale morph has whitish belly contrasting with otherwise dark brown plumage; dark morph is uniformly dark brown. Non-breeding adults show some barring on underparts in pale phase. JUVENILE: Underparts heavily barred brown and white. FIRST-WINTER: Like non-breeding adult, but has barring also on underwing in pale phase.

BEHAVIOUR: Similar to that of South Polar Skua.

④ South Polar Skua   *Catharacta maccormicki*   Salteador Polar

Length: 50–55 cm
Wingspan: 130–140 cm

Vagrant, but probably under-recorded as it is a regular trans-equatorial migrant in the Pacific.

IDENTIFICATION: A large, heavy skua with conspicuous white wing-flashes at the base of the primaries. Occurs in two colour phases: pale morph shows obvious contrast between light grey head and underparts, and dark brown upperparts; dark morph is uniformly dark brown except for pale, brown-streaked collar.

BEHAVIOUR: Kleptoparasitises other seabirds, displaying surprising agility for its bulk. Normal flight is direct, low over the water and with heavy, deliberate wingbeats.

PLATE 10

❶ Laughing Gull   *Larus atricilla*   Gaviota Reidora

Length: 39–46 cm
Wingspan: 102–107 cm

Regular migrant, mostly from October to May. Breeds in North and Central America and the Caribbean, some birds migrating to winter along the west coast of South America.

IDENTIFICATION: Similar to Franklin's Gull but slightly larger and generally darker on the upperparts with longer bill, which has a pronounced droop, flatter crown and longer legs. Adult Breeding: Similar to Franklin's, but in flight rather more pointed wings show predominantly black wing-tips. Adult Non-breeding: As adult breeding but pale-headed, lacking the partial hood of Franklin's. First-winter: As in adult non-breeding, hood less pronounced than in equivalent plumage of Franklin's, though displays indistinct black markings around ear-coverts. Underparts dusky compared with Franklin's, and in flight the black sub-terminal tail-band is unbroken, extending to the edge of the tail.

❷ Franklin's Gull   *Larus pipixcan*   Gaviota de Franklin

Length: 32–38 cm
Wingspan: 87–91 cm

Regular migrant, mostly from October to May. Breeds in North America, spending the northern winter on the west coast of South America.

IDENTIFICATION: A smallish gull. Adult Breeding: White underparts and tail with medium-grey mantle and upperwings. Black hood with bold white crescents above and below eye. Bill dark red. In flight shows equal amount of black and white at wing-tip. Adult Non-breeding: Differs from breeding adult in much reduced hood, with black only around and behind the eye. First-winter: Saddle dark grey; rest of upperparts and upperwings grey-brown; partial hood as in non-breeding adult. In flight, white tail has black subterminal band which does not extend to the edge of the tail as the outermost tail feathers are white.

❸ Grey-headed Gull   *Larus cirrocephalus*   Gaviota Cabecigris

Length: 39–42 cm
Wingspan: 100–115 cm

Vagrant: recorded once, in 1978, but possibly overlooked as common along the western coast of South America.

IDENTIFICATION: A medium-sized gull with grey underwings and prominent white flash on inner primaries in flight. Adult: White underparts and tail with medium-grey mantle and wings. Hood grey, similar in tone to wings; lack of crescents above and below pale eye is diagnostic. Bill dark red and relatively slender; legs red. Adult Non-breeding/Second-winter: As adult breeding but grey hood replaced by dark smudges above eye and on ear coverts, and red bill develops dark tip. Juvenile/First-winter/First-summer: Similar to juvenile but with paler head, greyer upperparts and whiter underparts. Second-winter/Second-summer: As adult non-breeding but has black terminal band on tail, some brown feathering on wings and a duller bill.

❹ Kelp Gull   *Larus dominicanus*   Gaviota Dominicana

Length: 54–65 cm
Wingspan: 128–142 cm

Vagrant: few records.

IDENTIFICATION: A large, rather heavily-built gull with a stout bill. Adult: All-white apart from black mantle and upperwings. In flight shows white trailing-edge to wings and small white 'windows' at wing-tips. Bill yellow with red spot; legs greenish-yellow. Juvenile: Dark brown with buff edges to flight and tail feathers; bill dark. First-winter/First-summer: Similar to juvenile but with paler head, greyer upperparts and whiter underparts. Second-winter/Second-summer: Head and underparts white, faintly streaked with brown; wings and mantle black with grey-brown coverts; bill dull yellow with indistinct orange spot; legs dull yellow.

VOICE: A harsh, repeated "*kree–ok*".

1

1f-w

4f-w

2

4

1

2n

2f-w

1n

3

1f-w

4f-w

4s-w

4

PLATE 11

❶ Red-billed Tropicbird   *Phaethon aethereus*   Ave Tropical

Length: 90–105 cm
Wingspan: 99–106 cm

Common resident; population estimated to be a few thousand pairs in about 30 colonies. Nests colonially in rocky crevices or on bare ground, breeding throughout the year.

IDENTIFICATION: ADULT: Large, mainly white seabird with a bright red bill, yellow legs and very long, white central tail-streamers (46–56 cm). Broad black eye-stripe extends back towards the nape. Upperparts have fine grey barring. In flight shows black primaries. JUVENILE: Similar to adult, but lacks the tail-streamers, has a yellow bill, and the black eye-stripes meet at the nape.

VOICE: A loud, shrill rattle, "*kree-kree-kree*".

BEHAVIOUR: Feeds by hovering and plunge-diving, usually far from land. Flight is graceful, alternating fluttering wingbeats with gliding. Often seen resting on the sea with the tail raised.

❷ Common Noddy   *Anous stolidus*   Gaviotín Cabeza Blanca

Length: 38–45 cm
Wingspan: 75–86 cm

Common resident; endemic subspecies *galapagensis*. Population estimated to be a few thousand pairs. Breeds throughout the archipelago in small colonies on sea cliffs just above the tideline.

IDENTIFICATION: The only entirely dark tern, with typical pointed wings, and wedge-shaped tail. Smaller and more elegant than Lava Gull. ADULT: Dark brown overall, except for whitish-grey forehead and crown, and white eyelids. In flight shows pale wing-bar on upperwing and dusky-grey centre to underwing. JUVENILE: Similar to adult, but lacks contrasting cap.

VOICE: Usually silent, but occasionally emits a low guttural growl.

BEHAVIOUR: Hovers above sea, often in large groups, sometimes accompanying pelicans, which may be used as a perch! Generally flies low over the sea, picking food from the surface; does not plunge-dive.

❸ Sooty Tern   *Sterna fuscata*   Gaviotín Negro

Length: 43–45 cm
Wingspan: 86–94 cm

Resident; breeding only on Darwin, where it is present in very large numbers. Seen only infrequently elsewhere in Galápagos.

IDENTIFICATION: Unmistakable; the only tern with contrasting black and white plumage. ADULT: Upperparts entirely black apart from white triangle on forehead; underparts white. In flight shows white outer tail-streamers. JUVENILE: Mostly sooty-brown, finely spotted white above, dusky below with paler belly.

VOICE: Noisy, with loud "*ker–wacky–wack*" call at breeding colony.

BEHAVIOUR: Very buoyant flight. Often seen feeding in large flocks, snatching food from the surface of the sea; does not plunge-dive.

PLATE 12

1 Black Tern *Chlidonias niger* Gaviota Negra

Length: 23–28 cm
Wingspan: 58–66 cm

Vagrant; one record of a dead immature bird.

IDENTIFICATION: A small, dark tern with a thin, dark red bill. ADULT BREEDING: Black head, neck and underparts, except for white vent and undertail. Upperwing dark grey; tail and underwing pale grey. ADULT NON-BREEDING: Pale grey above, white below, with dark shoulder-patch. Head white with black on crown extending to nape, ear-coverts and through eye. FIRST-WINTER: Similar to non-breeding adult, but upperparts show brownish tinges, especially on upperwing in flight.

BEHAVIOUR: Migrants usually feed in coastal waters, dipping down to take food from the surface, frequently hovering. Flight graceful and buoyant.

2 Common Tern *Sterna hirundo* Gaviotín Común

Length: 32–39 cm
Wingspan: 72–83 cm

Regular migrant in small numbers. Breeds in the northern hemisphere, the North American population wintering off Central and South America. Most Galápagos records have been during the northern winter.

IDENTIFICATION: A medium-sized tern, pale grey above and white below with a black cap and short red legs. ADULT BREEDING: Black cap extends from bill to nape. Bill red with a black tip. Long, forked tail reaches wing-tip when perched. In flight shows dark outer webs to primaries and dark trailing-edge to primaries on underwing. ADULT NON-BREEDING: As adult breeding but forehead white and bill all black. FIRST-WINTER: Like non-breeding adult, but has prominent dark carpal bar and dusky trailing-edge to secondaries.

BEHAVIOUR: A typical tern with light and buoyant flight. Feeds by plunge-diving from the air and surface-dipping.

3 Royal Tern *Sterna maxima* Gaviotín Real

Length: 45–51 cm
Wingspan: 100–135 cm

Regular migrant in small numbers, most records having been from the south of Isabela and Santa Cruz from January to March. Breeds in North America, the Caribbean and northern South America, some birds migrating to winter along the north-west coast of South America.

IDENTIFICATION: A large, stocky tern with a heavy, orange bill and black legs. ADULT BREEDING: Upperparts pale grey; underparts white. Black crown, extending from bill to nape. In flight shows white forked tail and dark trailing-edge to primaries on underwing. ADULT NON-BREEDING: Similar to adult breeding but lores, forehead and forecrown white, merging, with variable black spotting on crown, to shaggy black nape. FIRST-WINTER: Resembles non-breeding adult, but has dark brown markings on wings.

VOICE: A loud, harsh "*kee–reer*"

BEHAVIOUR: Could be mistaken for a gull due to its large size and powerful flight. When feeding, flies relatively high over the water and plunge-dives or surface-dips.

4 White Tern *Gygis alba* Gaviotín Blanco

Length: 25–30 cm
Wingspan: 76–80 cm

Vagrant; very few records. Breeds on tropical islands throughout the world.

IDENTIFICATION: Unmistakable; a small, very dainty, white tern with slightly upturned black bill and blue-grey legs. Graceful in flight, with almost translucent wings and a shallow-forked tail. ADULT: Plumage entirely white except for black eye-ring. JUVENILE: Similar to adult but back brownish-grey and shows dark smudges behind the eye and on the nape.

BEHAVIOUR: A tame and inquisitive species. Feeds by diving onto the surface of the sea.

PLATE 13

1 **Blue-winged Teal** *Anas discors* Cerceta Aliazul

Length: 39 cm — Vagrant; few records, mainly from coastal lagoons but also from ponds in the highlands, mostly during December to April.

IDENTIFICATION: A small, mainly brown dabbling duck with pale yellowish legs and feet; distinctive blue forewing and pale underwing in flight. MALE: Unmistakable in breeding plumage, with slate-grey head and large white facial crescent between eye and bill, and black undertail-coverts with white 'spot' on rear flanks. FEMALE/IMMATURE/ECLIPSE MALE: Brown with spotted underparts and faintly streaked face and neck with small, whitish loral spot; bill dark grey.

2 **Masked Duck** *Oxyura dominica* Malvasía Enmascarada

Length: 30–36 cm — Vagrant; one record of a pair with a duckling on El Junco Lake, San Cristóbal in December 1994.

IDENTIFICATION: A small, compact diving duck, readily told in flight by conspicuous white patch across centre of wing, and on water by long, pointed tail which is often raised at about 45°. MALE: Unmistakable in breeding plumage, with rufous body mottled with dark brown and black; black face; and blue bill tipped black. FEMALE/IMMATURE/ECLIPSE MALE: Brown with mottled underparts and buff head with black stripes through and below eye and on crown; bill bluish.

3 **Pied-billed Grebe** *Podilymbus podiceps* Somormujo

Length: 34 cm — Vagrant; recorded regularly, mainly on brackish lagoons, particularly on San Cristóbal, and may have bred.

IDENTIFICATION: The only grebe recorded. Told from other waterbirds by aquatic habits, frequently diving; small size; short-necked and large-headed appearance with very short tail; uniform grey-brown plumage with white undertail-coverts; and stout, pale bill which, during the breeding season, has a vertical black band.

4 **American Coot** *Fulica americana* Focha Americana

Length: 34–43 cm — Vagrant; first recorded in 1999. Breeds mainly in North and Central America and the West Indies, migrating to winter usually only as far south as Panamá.

IDENTIFICATION: A largish, plump rail, distinguished from similar Common Gallinule (see Plate 14) by lack of white flank-stripe and colour of frontal shield. ADULT: Plumage entirely slate-grey apart from white outermost undertail-coverts. White bill and frontal shield diagnostic, the bill having a broken reddish subterminal band.

e **5** **White-cheeked (or Galápagos) Pintail** *Anas bahamensis* Patillo

Length: 46 cm — Fairly common resident; endemic subspecies *galapagensis*. Breeds opportunistically throughout the year when conditions are favourable, nesting near the ground in waterside vegetation.

IDENTIFICATION: Unmistakable: a medium-sized, slender dabbling duck with white cheeks and throat, and black bill with red sides to base. In flight appears slender with long, pointed tail and conspicuous white cheeks and throat.

VOICE: Usually silent, although when calling, males make a low whistle and females utter a weak, descending series of quacks.

BEHAVIOUR: Usually found singly or in pairs or small groups near open wetlands, both near the coast and in the highlands. Usually feeds by dabbling and up-ending, although regularly dives for food in deep water.

6 **Black-bellied Whistling Duck** *Dendrocygna autumnalis* Guirirí

Length: 48–58 cm — Vagrant; one record from Isabela.

IDENTIFICATION: ADULT: Unmistakable: a medium-sized, mainly rufous-brown duck with red bill and legs, black underparts, grey head and upper-neck, and prominent white wing-flash. IMMATURE: Plumage similar to adult but bill and legs blue-grey.

PLATE 14

① Paint-billed Crake *Neocrex erythrops* Gallareta

Length: 18–20 cm

Scarce resident; found principally in agricultural areas, favouring dense, wetland vegetation although also occurs in damp woodlands and in dry pastures and thickets. Breeds from November to February.

IDENTIFICATION: A small, rather dark rail. ADULT: Upperparts olive-brown; underparts slate-grey with narrow white vertical bars on flanks; bill pale green with bright red base and black tip; legs and feet red. JUVENILE: Similar to adult but plumage generally duller and paler with dark bill lacking the red base.

VOICE: Song is a long, descending and gradually accelerating series of staccato notes followed by a few short churrs. Call is a frog-like "*qurrk*", either given singly or in a series.

BEHAVIOUR: Mainly crepuscular and very secretive. Rarely flies unless flushed.

E ② Galápagos Rail *Laterallus spilonotus* Pachay

Length: 15–16 cm

Uncommon resident; breeds from September to April. Population declining and range becoming increasingly restricted; now virtually confined to the highlands where it inhabits dense grassy vegetation, thickets and forests. Conservation Status: NEAR-THREATENED.

IDENTIFICATION: A tiny, dark, short-winged rail. ADULT: Upperparts dark chocolate-brown, finely spotted with white; underparts dark slate-grey to greyish-brown; eyes scarlet; legs and feet brown. JUVENILE: Similar to adult but plumage generally duller and slightly paler and lacks the white spots on the upperparts; eye dark.

VOICE: Gives a range of calls but typically a rapid "*chi–chi–chi–chirroo*".

BEHAVIOUR: Rather furtive, although can be very tame and sometimes inquisitive. Flight very weak and runs rather than flies when disturbed.

③ Sora (Rail) *Porzana carolina* Polluela Norteña

Length: 19–25 cm

Vagrant; three records, all of birds found dead. Normally favours freshwater, brackish and coastal marshes with emergent vegetation.

IDENTIFICATION: A small, plump rail with 'stubby' yellow or greenish-yellow bill. ADULT: Shows obvious black face 'mask'. JUVENILE/IMMATURE: Similar to adult but duller.

④ Common Gallinule (or Moorhen) *Gallinula chloropus* Gallinula

Length: 30–38 cm

Resident, mainly inhabiting brackish lagoons; breeds mostly from May to October.

IDENTIFICATION: A medium-sized, dark gallinule. ADULT: Generally dark blackish-grey, with distinctive broken white line along flanks, and white undertail-coverts; frontal shield and base of bill bright red and tip of bill yellow; legs and feet yellow, with upper part of tibia orange. JUVENILE: Much duller than adult, with pale brown underparts and greenish-brown bill, lacking the frontal shield; legs and feet olive-grey.

VOICE: Typically an explosive "*krrruk*", but also gives a range of sharp "*kik*" and "*kark*" calls.

BEHAVIOUR: Distinctive, jerky head movement when swimming.

⑤ American Purple Gallinule *Porphyrio martinica* Gallito Azul

Length: 27–36 cm

Vagrant; few records.

IDENTIFICATION: A medium-sized, rather slender gallinule. ADULT: Head, neck and underparts iridescent purplish-blue, with white undertail-coverts; upperparts olive-green; frontal shield pale blue; bill bright red at base with yellow tip; legs and feet yellow. JUVENILE: Much duller than adult with pale brown underparts; yellow-green bill with pale tip, lacking the frontal shield; and yellowish or brownish legs and feet.

PLATE 15

1 Greater Flamingo *Phoenicopterus ruber*   Flamenco

Length: *c.* 120 cm
Wingspan: *c.* 140 cm

Resident; sometimes treated as an endemic subspecies *glyphorhynchus*. Population estimated at between 400–500 birds. Breeds in small colonies from July to March, building mud nests in saltwater lagoons.

IDENTIFICATION: Unmistakable; a very large, long-necked, pink bird with distinctive 'kinked' bill. Neck extended in flight. ADULT: Wholly pink with conspicuous black flight feathers in flight. IMMATURE: As adult but plumage whitish.

VOICE: A series of rather goose-like "*ah–ah–ah* ..." calls.

BEHAVIOUR: Feeds in small groups in saltwater lagoons. Occasionally seen at sea flying from one island to another.

e 2 Great Blue Heron *Ardea herodias*   Garza Morena

Length: *c.* 95 cm
Wingspan: *c.* 175 cm

Resident, endemic subspecies *cognata*. Found in small numbers in coastal areas, particularly near lagoons. Breeds throughout the year, nesting singly close to the shore, usually in mangroves.

IDENTIFICATION: Unmistakable: a very large, long-necked, grey heron. ADULT: Upperparts pale grey; sides of neck violaceous-grey; head white with broad black line along side of crown extending to long crest; underparts mostly white with black spots on breast; legs and bill yellow, becoming pinkish during the breeding season. IMMATURE: Grey-brown with dark bill.

VOICE: Gives a harsh "*kraak*" in flight and a soft "*frawnk*" if disturbed near the nest.

BEHAVIOUR: Usually found singly. Sometimes flies with neck outstretched.

3 Tricolored Heron *Egretta tricolor*   Garza Tricolor

Length: *c.* 60 cm
Wingspan: *c.* 100 cm

Vagrant; recorded once.

IDENTIFICATION: A medium-sized heron with long, slender neck and relatively short legs. ADULT: Blue-grey upperparts, head and neck with white line running down front of neck; underparts and, in flight, underwing-coverts white; bill grey with dark tip; lores yellow. JUVENILE: Similar to adult but sides of head and neck rufous and mantle and wing-coverts tinged rufous.

4 Little Blue Heron *Egretta caerulea*   Garza Azul

Length: *c.* 65 cm
Wingspan: *c.* 100 cm

Vagrant; recorded once, in 1998.

IDENTIFICATION: A medium-sized, long-necked heron. ADULT: Uniform slate-blue plumage with purple or cinnamon wash to head and neck; bill blue-grey with dark tip; legs and feet black. JUVENILE/IMMATURE: White, blotched with variable amounts of blue-grey (see Plate 16).

PLATE 16

❶ Cattle Egret   *Bulbulcus ibis*   Garza (del Ganado) Bueyera

Length: *c.* 50 cm
Wingspan: *c.* 90 cm

Resident. First recorded in 1964 but breeding not proved until 1986; now well established, particularly in agricultural areas on the inhabited islands. Nests colonially in bushes or trees.

IDENTIFICATION: A medium-sized, short-necked and rather compact white heron with yellow bill and relatively short, dark green legs and feet which can appear black at a distance. In breeding plumage, develops rufous-buff plumes on the crown, nape, mantle and upper breast, and the legs become yellow and, for a short while, bright red.

VOICE: At breeding colony typically gives a harsh "*rick-rack*" call, although also has a range of other harsh calls including "*raa*", "*kraa*", "*thonk*" and "*kok*".

BEHAVIOUR: Usually found in loose flocks in agricultural areas feeding on invertebrates disturbed by livestock or tortoises, although sometimes seen near the coast, particularly around lagoons.

❷ Little Blue Heron   *Egretta caerulea*   Garza Azul

Length: *c.* 60 cm
Wingspan: *c.* 100 cm

Vagrant; recorded once, in 1998.

IDENTIFICATION: A medium-sized, long-necked heron. ADULT: Slate-blue (see Plate 15). JUVENILE: White with yellowish-green legs and feet and grey or pinkish bill with dark tip; lores usually grey. Dark tips to primaries diagnostic. IMMATURE: White plumage blotched with blue-grey; white feathers gradually replaced with blue-grey as bird matures.

❸ Snowy Egret   *Egretta thula*   Garcita Blanca

Length: *c.* 60 cm
Wingspan: *c.* 100 cm

Vagrant; recorded most years in small numbers, particularly in coastal areas.

IDENTIFICATION: A medium-sized, long-necked, white heron readily identified by combination of black bill with yellow lores and black legs with yellow feet.

❹ Great Egret   *Ardea alba*   Garza Blanca

Length: *c.* 80 cm
Wingspan: *c.* 150 cm

Resident. Found in small numbers in coastal areas, particularly near lagoons, and occasionally in open areas in the highlands. Nests colonially, usually in mangroves.

IDENTIFICATION: A large, long-necked, white heron with yellow bill and black legs and feet, the upper part of the leg sometimes becoming yellowish during the breeding season. Gape extending behind eye is diagnostic.

VOICE: At breeding colony gives a soft "*frawnk*" or a deep "*rhaa*" or "*rhoo*"; in flight sometimes gives a low-pitched "*krraak*".

BEHAVIOUR: Usually found singly away from the breeding colony.

PLATE 17

❺ Green Heron   *Butorides virescens*   Garza Verde

Length: 35 cm
Wingspan: 63 cm

Vagrant; recorded once, in 1996, from the highlands of Floreana.

IDENTIFICATION: A very small, compact heron. ADULT: Similar to Striated Heron (see Plate 17), but cheeks, breast and neck rufous. JUVENILE: Indistinguishable from juvenile Striated or Lava Heron until it begins to attain adult plumage.

PLATE 17

e **1** **Yellow-crowned Night-heron** *Nycticorax violaceus* Guaque; Garza Nocturna

Length: *c.* 60 cm
Wingspan: *c.* 100 cm

Fairly common resident; endemic subspecies *pauper*. Mainly found in coastal areas, breeding throughout the year and nesting close to the ground amongst mangrove roots or rocks and sometimes in caves.

IDENTIFICATION: A medium-sized, squat heron, with legs protruding beyond the tip of the tail in flight. ADULT: Unmistakable: generally dark grey with pale fringes to wing and back feathers; black head with white cheeks and yellow crown; legs yellow and bill black. IMMATURE: Similar to adult but plumage brown rather than grey and head pattern indistinct. JUVENILE: Dark brown with white or buff spots and streaks on upperparts, and creamy-white and brown streaks on underparts; lacks the head markings of adult. Underwings greyish.

VOICE: A range of calls but typically an often-repeated, rather high-pitched "*kwok*"; in flight gives a "*scalp*".

BEHAVIOUR: Mainly nocturnal, often seen flying from roost sites at dusk to feed; usually a solitary feeder but flocks can sometimes be found around coastal lagoons.

2 **Black-crowned Night-heron** *Nycticorax nycticorax* Garza Nocturna

Length: *c.* 60 cm
Wingspan: *c.* 100 cm

Vagrant; one record of an immature bird on Santa Cruz in 1971.

IDENTIFICATION: Similar in size and shape to Yellow-crowned Night-heron but posture typically rather more hunched with neck tucked into shoulders; in flight only tips of toes project beyond the tip of the tail. ADULT: Unmistakable: underparts, neck and face white; wings uniform pale grey; back and crown black; legs yellow and bill black. JUVENILE: Very similar to juvenile Yellow-crowned, but paler with more numerous and larger, buffy-white spots and streaks on upperparts, and darker streaking on underparts. Underwings whitish.

VOICE: Flight call is a hoarse, low-pitched "*kwark*".

3 **Striated Heron** *Butorides striatus* Garza Verde

Length: 35 cm
Wingspan: 63 cm

Uncommon resident, probably breeding throughout the year when conditions are suitable; nests usually solitary.

IDENTIFICATION: A very small, compact heron. ADULT: Back and wings greenish-grey, with wing coverts fringed brown; cheeks and sides of neck pale grey, contrasting with black crown; underparts pale grey with white line down front of neck and often with brownish wash to sides of lower neck and upper breast. Legs dull greyish-yellow, becoming bright yellow when breeding. JUVENILE: Indistinguishable from juvenile Lava Heron until it begins to attain adult plumage.

VOICE: Alarm call is a sharp "*keyow*", indistinguishable from Lava Heron.

BEHAVIOUR: Found in similar habitats to Lava Heron, but more often in freshwater habitats.

E **4** **Lava (or Galápagos) Heron** *Butorides sundevalli* Garza de Lava

Length: 35 cm
Wingspan: 63 cm

Common resident; considered by some authorities to be a subspecies of Striated Heron. Mainly found in coastal areas, breeding throughout the year when conditions are suitable; nests usually solitary, built low down in mangroves or under rocks.

IDENTIFICATION: A very small, compact heron. ADULT: Unmistakable: wholly blackish-grey with dull greyish-orange legs which become bright yellow or orange when breeding. JUVENILE: Predominantly brown, with whitish tips to wing-coverts and pale fringes to wing feathers; breast pale with brown streaking; crown dark; back uniform grey; cheeks and sides of neck washed brown. Indistinguishable from juvenile Striated Heron until it begins to attain adult plumage.

VOICE: Alarm call is a sharp "*keyow*".

BEHAVIOUR: Feeds in the shore zone.

5 **Green Heron**
Butorides virescens
text on page 64

PLATE 18

❶ Black-necked Stilt *Himantopus mexicanus* Tero Real

Length: 35–40 cm

Uncommon resident. Found in saline and freshwater habitats throughout the islands, breeding from December to June. This New World form is sometimes considered to be the same species as the Black-winged Stilt *H. himantopus* of the Old World.

IDENTIFICATION: A medium-sized, unmistakable wader with black wings, mantle, hindneck and crown; white underparts, rump and tail; and extremely long, pink legs which project well beyond the tip of the tail in flight. Sexes alike although females have brown cast to mantle.

VOICE: Gives a range of high-pitched piping calls, including "*kik-kik-kik...*", "*kek*" and "*kee-ack*".

❷ Black Turnstone *Arenaria melanocephala* Vuelvepiedras Negro

Length: 22–25 cm

Vagrant; one record from the highlands of San Cristóbal.

IDENTIFICATION: Size and shape as Ruddy Turnstone with similar wing-pattern in flight. Differs from Ruddy in having black head, throat and breast (although breeding adult has white spot at base of bill), and darker, greyish legs.

❸ Surfbird *Aphriza virgata* Chorlito de Rompientes

Length: 23–26 cm

Scarce migrant, mainly during the northern winter; confined to rocky coasts.

IDENTIFICATION: A smallish, rather stocky wader, similar in size and shape to the turnstones although bill blunt-tipped and not upturned; in flight lacks the turnstones' white rump. ADULT BREEDING: Head, neck and breast heavily streaked black extending to black chevrons on flanks; golden-buff markings on scapulars. ADULT NON-BREEDING AND JUVENILE: Similar to Black Turnstone but throat white and legs yellow; shows some black markings on flanks.

❹ Ruddy Turnstone *Arenaria interpres* Vuelve Piedras

Length: 21–26 cm

A common migrant, present throughout the year although most numerous from September to March; confined to the coast.

IDENTIFICATION: A smallish, rather stocky wader with relatively short, orange legs and short, slightly upturned bill. In flight shows distinctive variegated wing-pattern. ADULT BREEDING: Back and wings rufous; distinctive black and white facial pattern and black breast-band contrasting with unmarked white underparts; throat white. ADULT NON-BREEDING AND JUVENILE: Similar to, but duller than, breeding adult, with less rufous on upperparts and less distinct head-pattern.

VOICE: A staccato rattle "*tuk, tuk–e–tuk–tuk*".

BEHAVIOUR: Usually occurs in small flocks.

ⓔ ❺ American Oystercatcher *Haematopus palliatus* Ostrero

Length: 40–44 cm

Uncommon resident; endemic subspecies *galapagensis*. Population probably numbers around 200 pairs. Confined to rocky shores, sandy beaches and coastal lagoons; breeds mainly from October and March.

IDENTIFICATION: A large, unmistakable wader with black head and neck, dark brown upperparts, white underparts, long orange bill and rather short, pink legs. In flight shows prominent white wing-bar and white rump contrasting with black tail.

VOICE: A distinctive, shrill piping "*kleet*".

BEHAVIOUR: Usually found in pairs.

PLATE 19

1 **Wilson's Plover**   *Charadrius wilsonia*   Chorlo de Wilson

Length: 20 cm   Vagrant; one record of three birds on Floreana in May 1969.

IDENTIFICATION: Slightly larger than Semipalmated Plover, with a longer, heavier, black bill. ADULT BREEDING: Upperparts dark grey-brown, underparts white with broad black breast-band (brown in female). Brown and white head-pattern includes (male only) black forecrown. ADULT NON-BREEDING/JUVENILE/FIRST-WINTER: Resembles breeding female, but lacks any rufous tinges; upperparts more scaly in juvenile. **VOICE:** A high-pitched, short whistle: "*wheet*".

2 **Killdeer**   *Charadrius vociferus*   Playero Gritón

Length: 27 cm   Vagrant; one record from Isabela in February 1971.

IDENTIFICATION: A distinctive, medium-sized plover with black double breast-band and long tail. In flight shows bright chestnut rump and broad white wing-bar. ADULT: Upperparts dark brown, with rufous fringes in non-breeding plumage. JUVENILE: Similar to non-breeding adult, but has paler fringes. **VOICE:** A very loud, penetrating "*kill–dee*", uttered repeatedly.

3 **Semipalmated Plover**   *Charadrius semipalmatus*   Chorlitejo

Length: 18 cm   Fairly common migrant, most numerous from August to May, although present throughout the year, occurring in the shore zone.

IDENTIFICATION: A small plover, brown above with white collar, and white below with dark breast-band. Conspicuous white wing-bar in flight. ADULT BREEDING: Contrasting black and white head-pattern, black breast-band. Bill orange with black tip. ADULT NON-BREEDING: Black parts of breeding plumage replaced by dark brown and bill darker. JUVENILE: Similar to non-breeding adult, but with buff fringes to upperparts. **VOICE:** A plaintive, rising "*chew–ee*", accented on the second syllable. **BEHAVIOUR:** Usually found on sandy shorelines, but occasionally occurs in the highlands beside freshwater pools.

4 **Pacific Golden Plover**   *Pluvialis fulva*   Playero Dorado Siberiano

Length: 27 cm   Vagrant; one record.

IDENTIFICATION: Extremely similar to the American Golden Plover in all plumages. Pacific has slightly longer legs, shorter wings and heavier bill. ADULT BREEDING: White neck-stripe extends to side of belly, with smudgy-grey coloration. ADULT NON-BREEDING/JUVENILE/FIRST-WINTER: More golden, with less grey tones to upperparts and breast than American Golden Plover; supercilium buff. **VOICE:** A sharp "*chu–it*".

5 **American Golden Plover**   *Pluvialis dominica*   Playero Dorado Americana

Length: 27 cm   Vagrant; one record from Santa Cruz.

IDENTIFICATION: Both this and the very similar Pacific Golden Plover are daintier versions of the Black-bellied Plover, with longer legs and slimmer bill. ADULT BREEDING: Underparts jet-black. Upperparts spangled gold and black, with white neck-stripe. ADULT NON-BREEDING/JUVENILE/FIRST-WINTER: Rather plain with dark-grey upperparts flecked with gold; prominent white supercilium. **VOICE:** A clear, melancholy whistle, either a single or a double note.

6 **Black-bellied (or Grey) Plover**   *Pluvialis squatarola*   Playero Cabezón

Length: 29 cm   Regular migrant, recorded throughout the year. Occurs in small numbers, mostly on sandy beaches.

IDENTIFICATION: A plump, medium-sized wader with short, stout bill. ADULT BREEDING: Underparts jet-black from face to belly, separated from spangled grey and silver upperparts by broad white stripe on side of neck. ADULT NON-BREEDING/JUVENILE/FIRST-WINTER: Grey-brown upperparts, spotted white (buff in juvenile); pale-brown underparts. Distinctive black 'armpits' in flight. **VOICE:** Flight call is a loud, three-note whistle: "*pee–oo–wee*".

PLATE 20

❶ Willig *Catoptrophorus semipalmatus* Chorlitejo

Length: 33–41 cm   Regular migrant, occurring in the shore zone.

IDENTIFICATION: A large, plump wader with a heavy straight bill and longish blue-grey legs. Greyish overall, but with a striking black and white pattern on the open wing. ADULT BREEDING: Upperparts greyish-brown, lightly speckled black. Underparts white, with faint barring on breast and flanks. ADULT NON-BREEDING: Uniformly pale grey above and white below, with grey wash to breast. JUVENILE: Similar to non-breeding adult but upperparts slightly browner with buff fringes.

VOICE: Gives repeated shrill alarm call, "*weet, weet*" and loud triple flight call, "*will–will–willet*".

❷ Short-billed Dowitcher *Limnodromus griseus* Agujeta Piquicorta

Length: 25–29 cm   Uncommon migrant, occurring in the shore zone.

IDENTIFICATION: A medium-sized wader with short, greenish legs and a long, snipe-like bill. In flight shows a whitish back. ADULT BREEDING: Upperparts dark brown with narrow rufous fringes. Underparts rufous with whitish belly, barred and spotted on flanks. Tail finely barred. ADULT NON-BREEDING: Grey above and on breast; pale underparts. JUVENILE: Brighter than adult, lacking barring on underparts. Crown and upperparts broadly edged reddish-buff.

VOICE: A soft and rapid "*tu–tu–tu*".

❸ Hudsonian Godwit *Limosa haemastica* Aguja Café

Length: 36–42 cm   Vagrant; one record.

IDENTIFICATION: Smaller and shorter-legged than the Marbled Godwit, with a proportionately shorter, thinner bill, also slightly upturned. In flight, shows dark wing-linings, narrow white wing-bar, and black and white tail. ADULT BREEDING: Female is paler than male, with white blotching on underparts. ADULT NON-BREEDING: Dark grey upperparts and breast, pale belly and white supercilium. JUVENILE: Brownish-buff overall, with pale fringes on upperparts.

VOICE: A shrill, high-pitched "*whit*", often repeated.

❹ Whimbrel *Numenius phaeopus* Zarapito

Length: 40–46 cm   Regular migrant, found on rocky shores and lagoons; also around pools and in grassy areas in the highlands..

IDENTIFICATION: Unmistakable: the only large wader with a long, downcurved bill. Long-legged, with conspicuously striped crown. ADULT: Upperparts grey-brown; underparts paler, with fine streaking on breast. JUVENILE: Upperparts slightly darker than in adult, with buff spots and fringes on flight feathers.

VOICE: A very characteristic and far-carrying six or seven note trill: "*tu–tu–tu–tu–tu–tu*".

BEHAVIOUR: Found on rocky shores and lagoons; also around pools and in grassy areas in the highlands.

❺ Marbled Godwit *Limosa fedoa* Aguja Canela

Length: 42–48 cm   Scarce migrant, mainly between October and March, and found in the shore zone.

IDENTIFICATION: A large, richly mottled, brown wader with long legs and long, slightly uptilted bill. In flight shows cinnamon wing-bar. ADULT BREEDING: Upperparts speckled black and cinnamon; underparts pale chestnut, lightly streaked and barred dark brown. Face whitish, with dark crown and lores. ADULT NON-BREEDING/JUVENILE/FIRST-WINTER: Paler overall than adult breeding, lacking streaks and bars on underparts; juvenile has buff fringes to mantle feathers.

VOICE: A loud, harsh "*ker–whit*".

PLATE 21

❶ Lesser Yellowlegs · *Tringa flavipes* · Chorlo Chico

Length: 23–25 cm · Regular migrant, mostly between October and March, occurring in the shore zone.

IDENTIFICATION: Similar in structure to Greater Yellowlegs, but smaller and daintier, with thinner, proportionately shorter bill (shorter than length of tarsus). ADULT BREEDING: Differs from Greater in having largely unmarked flanks. ADULT NON-BREEDING/JUVENILE: Similar plumage to Greater, but less spotted on mantle and with finer breast streaking.

VOICE: A high-pitched "*tew–tew*", shorter and quieter than the call of Greater Yellowlegs.

❷ Greater Yellowlegs · *Tringa melanoleuca* · Chorlo Real

Length: 29–33 cm · Scarce migrant, occurring in the shore zone.

IDENTIFICATION: A fairly large, stocky wader with long, stout, slightly upturned bill (equal to or longer than length of tarsus) and long, bright orange-yellow legs. In flight shows white rump but no wing-bars. ADULT BREEDING: Head, throat and breast heavily streaked and flanks barred or with chevrons. Upperparts dark brown with white spots. ADULT NON-BREEDING: Similar to adult breeding but upperparts grey with finer white spotting; underparts white, with grey wash to breast and flanks. JUVENILE: Resembles non-breeding adult, but darker on mantle, and shows clear contrast between streaky breast and white belly.

VOICE: A loud, descending series of three or more notes: "*tew–tew–tew*".

❸ Pectoral Sandpiper · *Calidris melanotos* · Tin-Güín

Length: 20–23 cm · Vagrant; three records, two from the highlands of Santa Cruz and one from a coastal lagoon on Isabela during the northern winter.

IDENTIFICATION: A medium-sized wader with slightly decurved bill, strongly streaked breast sharply contrasting with white belly and, typically, upright stance. ADULT MALE BREEDING: Breast blackish with white mottling. ADULT FEMALE BREEDING: Smaller than male, with brown breast streaking. ADULT NON-BREEDING: Duller and greyer overall than in breeding plumage. JUVENILE: Upperparts brighter and more contrasting than adult, with buff and chestnut fringes, and more pronounced white supercilium.

❹ Buff-breasted Sandpiper · *Tryngites subruficollis* · Correlimos Canelo

Length: 18–20 cm · Vagrant; one record.

IDENTIFICATION: A medium-sized wader, with short, dark bill and shortish orange-yellow legs. The strong buff tones of face and underparts, together with the black 'button' eye in the plain face, are distinctive at all ages. JUVENILE: distinguished from adult by more scaly appearance to the dark brown upperparts.

BEHAVIOUR: Favours areas of short grass.

❺ Stilt Sandpiper · *Micropalama himantopus* · Correlinos Tarsilargo

Length: 18–23 cm · Vagrant; few records during the northern winter.

IDENTIFICATION: Resembles a long-legged Calidris sandpiper (see Plates 22 and 23), with a long, slightly decurved bill. In flight shows white rump but no wing-bars. ADULT BREEDING: Very distinctive, with rufous ear-coverts and crown-stripes, white supercilium and strongly barred underparts. ADULT NON-BREEDING: Greyer above and paler below than in adult breeding, lacking any strong markings. JUVENILE: Upperparts dark brown with rufous fringes on mantle and pale edges to wing-coverts and tertials.

PLATE 22

❶ Red Knot *Calidris canutus* Playero Pecho Rufo

Length: 23–25 cm Vagrant; one record from Floreana in 1969.

IDENTIFICATION: A dumpy, medium-sized wader, with a fairly short, straight bill and short, greenish legs. In flight shows pale grey rump. ADULT BREEDING: Brick-red underparts and a mixture of black and chestnut on upperparts. ADULT NON-BREEDING: Underparts white with grey wash on breast; upperparts grey with narrow white fringes to feathers. JUVENILE: Like non-breeding adult, but has a buffish tinge to the underparts and broader pale fringes to feathers on upperparts.

❷ Sanderling *Calidris alba* Playero Común

Length: 20–21 cm Common migrant, particularly during the northern winter, confined to the shore zone.

IDENTIFICATION: A very active small wader, distinctively pale in non-breeding plumage, with short black bill and legs. Runs energetically along the tideline. ADULT BREEDING: Head, mantle and breast rusty-red; underparts white. ADULT NON-BREEDING/FIRST-WINTER: Very pale grey above, with black shoulder-patch, and pure white below. JUVENILE: Mantle chequered black and white; creamy wash on breast and flanks.

VOICE: A sharp "*krit*", often repeated.

❸ Spotted Sandpiper *Actitis macularia* Correlino

Length: 18–20 cm Regular migrant; most records during the northern winter from the shore zone.

IDENTIFICATION: A small, active wader with constantly bobbing tail, shortish olive-yellow legs and medium-length bill; flies on stiff, bowed wings with a curious stuttering action. ADULT BREEDING: Strikingly plumaged, with white underparts liberally sprinkled with black spots, and finely barred, olive-brown upperparts. Bill orange with black tip. ADULT NON-BREEDING/ JUVENILE: Plain upperparts and unspotted white underparts, extending up side of breast to form a white shoulder patch.

VOICE: High, piping "*peet–weet–weet*" notes, usually given in flight.

❹ Wandering Tattler *Heteroscelus incanus* Errante

Length: 26–29 cm Common migrant; found throughout the year on rocky coasts.

IDENTIFICATION: A rather plain, medium-sized wader, with a stout, straight bill, white supercilium and short, yellow legs. ADULT BREEDING: Dark-grey above, heavily barred below. ADULT NON-BREEDING/JUVENILE: Underparts unbarred, the pale grey breast contrasting with the white belly.

VOICE: A clear 8–10-note trill, all on the same pitch.

❺ Solitary Sandpiper *Tringa solitaria* Playero Solitario

Length: 18–21 cm Occasional migrant; mostly recorded around small pools in the highlands from December to February.

IDENTIFICATION: Body shape and head pattern recall Lesser Yellowlegs, but smaller, with much darker upperparts and shorter, olive legs. Also has thicker bill and white eye-ring. ADULT BREEDING: Dark brown upperparts, finely spotted white. Head, neck and breast streaked blackish. ADULT NON-BREEDING: Plain, dark grey upperparts and breast, less spotted than breeding adult. JUVENILE: As non-breeding adult but upperparts spotted buff.

VOICE: A high "*pee–weet*" or "*pee–wee–weet*".

PLATE 23

1 **Least Sandpiper** *Calidris minutilla* Playero Enano

Length: 13–15 cm Regular migrant, found in small numbers throughout the year, especially from October to April, on the shoreline or beside pools.

IDENTIFICATION: A tiny wader, the smallest of the *Calidris* sandpipers, and most readily distinguished from the others in all plumages by its yellowish (not black) legs, thin and slightly downturned bill, and frequently 'hunched' posture. The upperparts are also generally darker than the other species.

VOICE: A high-pitched, drawn-out "*kreee*".

2 **Semipalmated Sandpiper** *Calidris pusilla* Playero Semipalmeado

Length: 13–15 cm Vagrant, recorded occasionally during the northern winter, and occurring in the shore zone.

IDENTIFICATION: Slightly larger than Least Sandpiper, with straighter, thicker bill, black legs and generally paler coloration. Very similar to Western Sandpiper, but bill shorter and blunter, lacking 'drooping' tip. ADULT BREEDING: Upperparts brownish-grey, with very little rufous on head and mantle. Scapulars dark-centred with pale grey edges. Breast and flanks finely streaked dark; belly and under-tail white. ADULT NON-BREEDING/FIRST-WINTER: Plain grey-brown above with darker crown and eye-stripe. Underparts white with grey wash to sides of breast. JUVENILE: Upperparts more contrasting than in adult, with rufous tones to crown and mantle; fairly prominent white supercilium.

VOICE: A low, short "*churck*".

3 **Western Sandpiper** *Calidris mauri* Playero Occipital

Length: 14–17 cm Vagrant; recorded most years during the northern winter, in small numbers, and occurring in the shore zone.

IDENTIFICATION: Similar in size and posture to Semipalmated Sandpiper, but bill longer, finer and slightly downcurved at the tip. In breeding and juvenile plumage shows more rufous on head and mantle. ADULT BREEDING: Generally more contrasting than Semipalmated, with bright rufous tones to crown, ear-coverts and scapulars. Neck, breast and flanks heavily streaked black, often extending to belly and undertail. ADULT NON-BREEDING/FIRST-WINTER: Plumage virtually indistinguishable from Semipalmated, though usually the cold grey tones predominate. JUVENILE: Brighter than Semipalmated, showing marked contrast between rufous upper scapulars and grey lower scapulars; crown buff-grey, streaked brown; breast has pale orange-buff wash.

VOICE: High-pitched, thin "*jeet*", very different from call of Semipalmated.

4 **White-rumped Sandpiper** *Calidris fuscicollis* Playero de Rabadilla Blanca

Length: 15–18 cm Vagrant; only a handful of records, from Fernandina and Floreana.

IDENTIFICATION: Similar in size and structure to Baird's Sandpiper, with long wings extending well beyond the tail when at rest. Greyer overall than Baird's with slightly more drooping black bill, usually showing a pale base to the lower mandible. In flight shows prominent white uppertail-coverts. ADULT NON-BREEDING/FIRST-WINTER: Upperparts grey-brown, lacking buff tones of Baird's, but showing similar pale fringes to the mantle and wing-coverts. Breast lightly streaked grey; rest of underparts white. JUVENILE: Usually more brightly coloured than Baird's, with rich chestnut tones to scapulars and dark-streaked crown, bordered by prominent white supercilium; breast and flanks streaked black under a grey wash.

VOICE: Flight call differs from Baird's: a thin, high-pitched "*cheeet*".

5 **Baird's Sandpiper** *Calidris bairdii* Playero de Baird

Length: 14–17 cm Vagrant, seen very occasionally on migration between Arctic breeding grounds and South American wintering areas, occurring in the shore zone.

IDENTIFICATION: A small, fairly short-billed wader lacking distinctive plumage characteristics, but its long wings give it an attenuated shape on the ground, similar to that of White-rumped Sandpiper. ADULT NON-BREEDING/FIRST-WINTER: Upperparts and breast-band greyish-brown with buff tones to head and breast. Mantle and wing-coverts show pale fringes, giving a slightly scaly appearance. JUVENILE: Similar to non-breeding adult but upperparts more strongly scaly.

VOICE: A low, trilling "*preeet*".

PLATE 24

❶ Red (or Grey) Phalarope   *Phalaropus fulicaria*   Falaropo Rojo

Length: 20–22 cm
Wingspan: 37–40 cm

Regular migrant, recorded regularly during the northern autumn and winter, mainly at sea. Almost certainly under-recorded due to its similarity to the much commoner Red-necked Phalarope.

IDENTIFICATION: Slightly larger and more bulky than Red-necked Phalarope, with shorter and thicker bill. ADULT FEMALE BREEDING: Black crown, white face and brick-red neck and underparts; mantle black with bright buff fringes. ADULT MALE BREEDING: Similar to breeding female, but duller and smaller. ADULT NON-BREEDING/FIRST-WINTER: Totally different from breeding plumage: pale grey above and all-white below, with black hindcrown and eye-patch. JUVENILE: Upperparts similar to breeding male but neck, breast and flanks buffy-pink and belly white. Usually shows a dark smudge behind the eye.

VOICE: Call is a short, sharp "*pik*".

BEHAVIOUR: Feeds in similar fashion to Red-necked Phalarope, frequently spinning to obtain prey.

❷ Red-necked Phalarope   *Phalaropus lobatus*   Falaropo Norteño

Length: 18–19 cm
Wingspan: 31–34 cm

Common migrant, particularly between August and April, with large flocks often occurring between the southern and central islands from December to January. Found at sea or on saltwater lagoons.

IDENTIFICATION: The smallest and daintiest phalarope; thin-necked and very thin-billed. As with all phalaropes, the male is less brightly coloured than the female in breeding plumage, reflecting their reversed roles in incubation and rearing young. ADULT FEMALE BREEDING: Bright chestnut-red sides to neck; slate-grey crown, face, sides of neck and breast; white throat and eye-spot; dark mantle, with bright buff lateral stripes. ADULT MALE BREEDING: Similar to breeding female but duller. ADULT NON-BREEDING/FIRST-WINTER: Predominantly grey above and white below, with black crown and eye-patch (usually slightly wider than in Red Phalarope, which is very similar in this plumage). Upperparts more contrasting than in Red Phalarope, with whitish fringes forming stripes along edge of mantle and scapulars. In flight shows darker central uppertail-coverts than Red. JUVENILE: Resembles non-breeding adult, but dark brown above and buffy-pink below.

VOICE: Call is a shrill "*kip*", reminiscent of Sanderling.

BEHAVIOUR: Unlike other waders, phalaropes are normally seen swimming rather than on land. Food is picked from the water surface, disturbed by the bird's rapid spinning motion. Highly gregarious and often extremely tame.

❸ Wilson's Phalarope   *Phalaropus tricolor*   Falaropo de Wilson

Length: 20–22 cm
Wingspan: 37–40 cm

Regular migrant; mainly from August to December. Unlike the other phalaropes, this species is usually found on coastal lagoons and occasionally inland lakes.

IDENTIFICATION: The largest phalarope, with long legs, and a long, straight and very thin bill. Frequently seen on land, where it resembles a pot-bellied Lesser Yellowlegs. ADULT FEMALE BREEDING: Unmistakable, with bold black band extending from bill through eye and down sides of neck, becoming reddish-chestnut; upperparts grey with chestnut bands. ADULT MALE BREEDING: Similar to breeding female but chestnut plumage replaced by dark brown. ADULT NON-BREEDING/FIRST-WINTER: Predominantly pale grey above and white below; legs are bright yellow (black in breeding plumage). JUVENILE: Resembles breeding male, but without brown neck-band; breast buff.

VOICE: Usually silent, but occasionally gives a soft croaking note in flight.

BEHAVIOUR: Rarely reported at sea. Like the other phalaropes, gregarious and confiding.

PLATE 25

E **①** Galápagos Hawk *Buteo galapagoensis* Gavilán de Galápagos

Length: *c*. 55 cm
Wingspan: *c*. 120 cm

Resident and sedentary. Found on most of the islands and occurring in all habitats from the coast to the highlands. Only breeds in drier areas in the lowlands, nesting throughout the year with a peak in activity in June and July. Population much reduced in recent years and now only about 130 breeding territories known. Conservation Status: **VULNERABLE.**

IDENTIFICATION: The only regularly occurring diurnal raptor, readily identified by broad wings and dark plumage. Sexes alike, although females appreciably larger than males. ADULT: Plumage dark sooty-brown; tail grey with inconspicuous blackish bands; legs and cere yellow. Flight feathers noticeably paler than rest of wing in flight. JUVENILE: Blackish-brown above, heavily mottled with buff; underparts pale buff, spotted and streaked brown; tail pale buff with narrow black bands.

VOICE: Gives a range of calls, but typically a far-carrying *"kee–kee–kee..."*.

BEHAVIOUR: Often seen soaring on updraughts and occasionally hovers. Feeds both by predation and scavenging. Females mate with more than one male, all birds helping to rear the young.

② Osprey *Pandion haliaetus* Aquila Pescadora

Length: *c*. 60 cm
Wingspan: *c*. 150 cm

Vagrant; recorded annually in small numbers, mainly between June and January.

IDENTIFICATION: A large, long-winged raptor with unmistakable combination of white underparts and brown upperparts; conspicuous black line through eye contrasts with white throat and pale crown; legs grey. In flight, underwings pale with obvious dark mark in carpal area; wings are held noticeably angled and often rather arched, reminiscent of a large gull.

BEHAVIOUR: Feeds exclusively on fish which are caught by plunge-diving, feet-first.

③ Peregrine *Falco peregrinus* Alcón Peregrino

Length: 39–50 cm
Wingspan: 95–115 cm

Vagrant; recorded annually in small numbers, mainly between November and March.

IDENTIFICATION: The only falcon recorded; a powerful flier, with pointed, rather broad-based wings and slow, stiff wingbeats, often appearing quite stocky. Sexes alike, although females appreciably larger than males. ADULT: Upperparts blue-grey; underparts white, narrowly barred grey; crown black, extending to prominent moustachials which contrast with white throat; legs, cere and eye-ring yellow. JUVENILE/IMMATURE: Similar to adult but browner overall with streaked rather than barred breast.

BEHAVIOUR: Feeds principally on birds which are pursued at speed and caught in flight, often following a stoop from a great height.

PLATE 26

1 **Common Nighthawk** *Chordeiles minor* Aguaitacamino Migratorio

Length: 24 cm
Wingspan: 38 cm

Scarce migrant; recorded occasionally in small numbers.

IDENTIFICATION: The only nightjar recorded, appearing rather long-winged and falcon-like in flight. In flight, prominent oval-shaped white patch in primaries is diagnostic. Upperparts generally brownish-grey with buff and white streaks and spots; underparts finely barred blackish-brown and whitish-buff. Throat patch white, particularly noticeable in male, although sexes otherwise alike.

BEHAVIOUR: Mainly nocturnal, feeding in flight; most likely to be seen at dawn and dusk. During the day rests on the ground and occasionally on posts.

e **2** **Barn Owl** *Tyto alba* Lechuza Blanca; Lechuza de Campanarios

Length: 26 cm
Wingspan: 68 cm

Uncommon resident; endemic subspecies *punctatissima*. Population estimated at *c.* 9,000 birds. Most numerous in the lowlands, where breeding has been recorded throughout the year. Also occurs in the highlands where breeding takes place mainly from November to May. Nests in cavities, mainly in or close to the ground but sometimes in holes in trees.

IDENTIFICATION: A medium-sized owl identified by combination of greyish golden-brown upperparts with small white spots, dusky underparts with faint black spotting, heart-shaped facial disc and dark eyes. In flight, underwings appear white.

VOICE: A rather high-pitched, hissing "*shrreeee*", although not often heard.

BEHAVIOUR: Mostly nocturnal, although sometimes seen hunting on the ground or from a perch during early morning and late evening; flies with slow, deep wingbeats and occasional glides. Sometimes found roosting during the day in buildings.

e **3** **Short-eared Owl** *Asio flammeus* Lechuza de Campo

Length: 34–42 cm
Wingspan: 90–105 cm

Uncommon resident; endemic subspecies *galapagoensis*. Population estimated at *c.* 9,000 birds. Found throughout the islands in a range of habitats, breeding from November to May and nesting mainly on the ground.

IDENTIFICATION: A fairly large, rather long-winged, brown owl with short, often inconspicuous, ear-tufts. Upperparts heavily mottled and streaked dark brown and buff; wings dark brown with buff spots; underparts slightly paler than upperparts with brown streaking, heaviest on the breast; facial disc dusky brown, bordered with narrow black and white lines; eyes yellow. In flight, underwings pale with black crescent in carpal area and black wing-tips. Sexes alike, although females appreciably larger than males.

VOICE: Generally silent, but during the breeding season gives a barking "*chef–chef–chef...*" alarm call, and, when displaying a "*whoo–whoo–whoo...*".

BEHAVIOUR: Most active during the early morning and late evening, quartering the ground with slow, deep wingbeats, somewhat reminiscent of a harrier. Tends to feed nocturnally in areas where Galápagos Hawk is present.

PLATE 27

1 **Belted Kingfisher** *Megaceryle alcyon* Martín Pescador Migratorio

Length: 28–33 cm | Annual migrant visitor, in small numbers, mainly between October and March. Breeds in North America, wintering chiefly in Central America.

IDENTIFICATION: Unmistakable; the only kingfisher recorded in Galápagos. Stockily built, with large, crested head and strong, dagger-like bill. Adults are blue-grey above, with a broad white collar. Underparts mainly white with, in male, a single blue-grey breast-band and in female an additional rufous band across the upper belly, extending to the flanks. Juveniles resemble adults, but have rufous tones to the breast-band.

VOICE: A very noisy species, with a harsh rattle "*kek–kek–kek–kek*".

BEHAVIOUR: Perches or hovers over water, plunging head first to catch fish.

2 **Eared Dove** *Zenaida auriculata* Paloma Sabanera

Length: 22–28 cm | Vagrant; recorded only once. Occurs throughout South America.

IDENTIFICATION: Larger than Galápagos Dove, with more uniform coloration. Upperparts olive-brown, with black spots on wings. Head and underparts pinkish-buff, with pale grey crown and black streaks behind and below the eye. Tail pointed, with outer feathers edged white and grey. Legs red.

3 **Feral Pigeon** *Columba livia* Paloma Bravía

Length: 31–34 cm | A fairly common, introduced resident occurring around human habitation, although recently eliminated from Santa Cruz.

IDENTIFICATION: The familiar pigeon of cities worldwide, whose ancestor is the wild Rock Dove. Occurs in many colour variations, some birds retaining the predominantly grey plumage of the Rock Dove, with double black wing-bar and purple-green iridescent neck and upper-breast, others having brown, black or white elements in numerous permutations.

E **4** **Galápagos Dove** *Zenaida galapagoensis* Paloma de Galápagos

Length: 18–23 cm | A generally common resident, though less so on Floreana, San Cristóbal and Santa Cruz. Found chiefly in the arid zone, where breeds from February to June, soon after the onset of rains, nesting on the ground, beneath lava or cacti. Two subspecies are recognised: *galapagoensis* (all islands except Darwin and Wolf) and *exsul* (Darwin and Wolf).

IDENTIFICATION: Unmistakable; the only dove likely to be encountered away from human habitation. ADULT: Head, neck and breast reddish-brown, belly buffish. Distinctive pattern on ear-coverts: a white stripe bordered by black lines. Iridescent bronze-green patch on side of neck. Scapulars and wing-coverts black-spotted with white edging. Eye-ring bright blue; legs red. JUVENILE: Similar to adult but plumage generally duller.

VOICE: Displaying males have a very deep, soft, cooing call.

BEHAVIOUR: Often very confiding.

PLATE 28

① **Dark-billed Cuckoo**   *Coccyzus melacoryphus*   Cuclillo

Length: 27 cm
Resident, fairly common on Isabela, Fernandina, Santa Cruz, San Cristóbal and Floreana but less common on Santiago and Pinzón.

IDENTIFICATION: A slim cuckoo, with a long tail and black, slightly decurved bill. ADULT: Greyish-brown above, buff below. Head dark grey, with blackish mask behind eye. Tail bronze above, black with white tips below. JUVENILE: Similar to adult but generally duller, with buff tips to wing-coverts, and no white tips to underside of tail.
VOICE: A low chuckle, "*cu–cu–cu–cu–culp–culp–culop*".
BEHAVIOUR: A secretive species, more often heard than seen, and usually glimpsed disappearing into undergrowth.

② **Black-billed Cuckoo**   *Coccyzus erythrophalmus*   Cuclillo Pico Negro

Length: 30 cm
Vagrant; a single record of a dead immature in 1970. Breeds in eastern North America and winters in north-west South America.

IDENTIFICATION: Slightly larger than Dark-billed Cuckoo, though similar in structure. ADULT: Upperparts brown, underparts white. Head the same colour as the mantle, lacking Dark-billed's mask, bill black; prominent red eye-ring. Undertail grey with narrow white tips. JUVENILE: Underparts tinged buff, but always whiter than Dark-billed. Eye-ring pale yellow. Undertail paler than that of adult.

③ **Smooth-billed Ani**   *Crotophaga ani*   Garrapatero Común

Length: 35 cm
Fairly common introduced resident, occurring in the highlands of Isabela, Santa Cruz, Floreana and Santiago.

IDENTIFICATION: Unmistakable, apart from close similarity to Groove-billed Ani (differences from which are described under that species). The only large, entirely black landbird found in Galápagos. ADULT: Plumage glossy-black. Wings broad and relatively short; tail very long, broadening towards the end. Bill very big, black and smooth, flattened laterally with a high arch to the upper mandible, curving down to the forehead. JUVENILE: Similar to adult but plumage generally browner and bill smaller.
VOICE: Has several calls, including a whining, ascending whistle and a harsh two-note alarm, repeated several times.
BEHAVIOUR: Gregarious, seen in small flocks, often in the vicinity of cattle where they feed on insects which they flush.

④ **Groove-billed Ani**   *Crotophaga sulcirostris*   Garrapatero Asurcado

Length: 32 cm
The status of this species is uncertain, owing to confusion with the Smooth-billed Ani. A few substantiated records apparently exist.

IDENTIFICATION: In general shape and plumage, indistinguishable from Smooth-billed Ani. However, the bill, although still heavy, is noticeably smaller, and in particular lacks the protruding arch on the upper mandible. At close range, grooves on the upper mandible may be visible, though they are lacking in juveniles.
VOICE: A liquid "*whee–hoo*", accented on the first syllable, a clucking note, and various other calls.
BEHAVIOUR: Similar to that of Smooth-billed Ani.

PLATE 29

1 Chimney Swift *Chaetura pelagica* Vencejo de Chimenea

Length: 13 cm — Vagrant, recorded only once. Breeds in eastern North America, wintering in western South America.

IDENTIFICATION: A small, dark swift with curved wings, narrowing slightly as they join the cigar-shaped body, and short, square tail. Its flight is fast and direct, very different from that of the hirundines.

E 2 Galápagos Martin *Progne modesta* Golondrina de Galápagos

Length: 15 cm — Uncommon resident. Present on the central and southern islands of the archipelago in small numbers, most numerous on Isabela, occurring chiefly in the highlands. Probably breeds during the warm/wet season, nests and breeding adults having been recorded in March.

IDENTIFICATION: The only all-dark hirundine apart from the uncommon Purple Martin. ADULT MALE: Dark blue overall, with broad, pointed wings and slightly forked tail. ADULT FEMALE/JUVENILE: Sooty-black above and dark brown below, usually appearing all-dark in flight.

VOICE: A short, warbling song, a twittering flight call "*cher–cher*", and a high-pitched alarm call are the most frequently heard vocalisations.

BEHAVIOUR: Flight action consists of alternating flaps and glides.

3 Purple Martin *Progne subis* Golondrina de Iglesias

Length: 19 cm — Infrequent visitor in small numbers, most often on Española and Santa Cruz. Possibly overlooked due to similarity to Galápagos Martin.

IDENTIFICATION: Larger and bulkier than Galápagos Martin with similar flight action. ADULT MALE: Plumage closely resembles that species, but has small white patch of feathers on sides of lower back, although this is usually concealed. ADULT FEMALE AND JUVENILE: Duller than male, with sooty-grey upperparts and contrasting pale grey underparts, and faint streaking on the breast and flanks. Distinguished from Galápagos Martin by paler breast.

BEHAVIOUR: Flight similar to that of Galápagos Martin.

4 Barn Swallow *Hirundo rustica* Golondrina de Horquilla

Length: 18 cm — Uncommon migrant, occurring mostly during the northern winter. Breeds throughout North America, migrating to South America.

IDENTIFICATION: Typical hirundine with long, deeply forked tail in adult. ADULT: Head and upperparts dark blue, forehead and throat chestnut, underparts cinnamon, with blue breast-band. In flight shows white spots on spread tail. JUVENILE: Duller and browner than adult; tail lacks long streamers, but still noticeably forked.

BEHAVIOUR: Has characteristic elegant, swooping flight, often low over the ground or water.

5 Bank Swallow (or Sand Martin) *Riparia riparia* Golondrina Parda

Length: 12 cm — Vagrant or scarce migrant, reported chiefly from the eastern islands. Breeds widely throughout North America, wintering in South America.

IDENTIFICATION: A small brown and white hirundine with a short, square tail, unlike any other member of the family found in Galápagos. Upperparts mouse-brown, underparts white except for a brown breast-band, narrowest in the middle. Tail very slightly forked, but looks square when spread.

BEHAVIOUR: Typical graceful and rapid flight of a hirundine, but more direct than that of Barn Swallow. Usually feeds over water.

6 Cliff Swallow *Petrochelidon pyrrhonota* Golondrina Risquera

Length: 13 cm — Vagrant; only a few records. **IDENTIFICATION:** Shorter than Barn Swallow, largely because square tail lacks streamers. In flight the pale rump also helps to distinguish it from this species. ADULT: Upperparts blue-black, with paler hindneck. Buff forehead contrasts with dark blue crown; sides of head and throat chestnut except for dark central throat patch. Underparts greyish-white. JUVENILE: duller than adult, with pale throat and dark forehead.

BEHAVIOUR: Similar to Barn Swallow, though has more soaring flight when feeding.

PLATE 30

e **1** **Vermilion Flycatcher** *Pyrocephalus rubinus*   Pajaro Brujo

Length: 14 cm

Common resident, breeding on all the main islands, mostly in the highlands. Two endemic subspecies occur: *nanus* which is found on all the larger islands except for San Cristóbal; and *dubius* which is confined to San Cristóbal and which is now very rare or possibly even extinct. The two forms are sometimes treated as endemic species and referred to as Galápagos Vermilion Flycatcher and San Cristóbal Vermilion Flycatcher respectively. Breeds during the warm/ wet season from December to May, nesting in trees and bushes.

IDENTIFICATION: Smaller and daintier than Large-billed Flycatcher. ADULT MALE: Unmistakable, with brilliant red crown and underparts, black mask and upperparts. ADULT FEMALE AND JUVENILE: Brown above and yellow below, with a whitish supercilium and pale throat and chin; lacks wing-bars.

The subspecies *dubius* differs from *nanus* in being slightly smaller and generally paler in all plumages

VOICE: During display flight, male has tinkling "*pitty–see, pitty–see*" song, interspersed with bill-snapping.

BEHAVIOUR: Typical flycatcher, chasing insects in the air and foraging on the ground.

2 **Eastern Kingbird** *Tyrannus tyrannus*   Pitirre Americanó

Length: 22 cm   Vagrant; two records in 1983 and 1997.

IDENTIFICATION: A stocky flycatcher, with an upright posture when perched. Adult has a black head, slate-grey upperparts, white underparts washed pale grey across the breast, and a black tail with a distinctive white terminal band. Juvenile is browner above, including the head, and has a darker breast.

E **3** **Large-billed (or Galápagos) Flycatcher** *Myiarchus magnirostris*

Length: 16 cm   Papamoscas

Common resident, occurring on all the islands except Darwin, Wolf and Genovesa. Commonest in the lowlands, though also found in the highlands. Breeds during the warm/wet season, from December to May, nesting in trees and bushes.

IDENTIFICATION: Head and upperparts brownish-grey; chin, throat and breast grey; belly pale yellow, less bright than that of female Vermilion Flycatcher. Closed wing shows a faint double wing-bar. Bill quite thick and black.

VOICE: A liquid "*wheet–wheet–wheet*" call and a melodious song.

BEHAVIOUR: Extremely tame and inquisitive.

PLATE 31

❶ Blackpoll Warbler   *Dendroica striata*   Reinita Rayada

Length: 14 cm   Vagrant; a single record in 1976.

IDENTIFICATION: ADULT MALE: In breeding plumage has black cap, white cheeks, bold black streaks on olive-grey upperparts, white underparts and two white wing-bars. FEMALE: Upperparts olive-grey, including crown; dingy white underparts, with fainter streaking than male; and distinct double wing-bars. JUVENILE: Similar to female, but throat and breast yellowish.

❷ Bananaquit   *Coereba flaveola*   Reinita Común

Length: 15 cm   Vagrant; one record.

IDENTIFICATION: A small, active bird with a sharp-pointed, decurved bill and rather short tail. Unlikely to be confused with any other species in Galápagos. ADULT: Upperparts and tail dark olive with a pale yellow rump; crown and eye-stripe black, separated by a long, white supercilium; throat and upper breast grey; rest of underparts lemon yellow. JUVENILE: Duller than adult, with less conspicuous supercilium.

BEHAVIOUR: Feeds energetically on fruits and nectar; often very tame.

❸ Red-eyed Vireo   *Vireo olivaceus*   Julián Chiuí Ojirajo

Length: 11 cm   Vagrant; few records.

IDENTIFICATION: Recalls a large, thick-billed warbler, with distinctive head pattern. ADULT: Mantle and tail dark olive-brown, underparts pale buffy-white; crown blue-grey, bordered with black line; supercilium white, contrasting with black eye-stripe. The red eye is only visible at close range. JUVENILE: Similar to adult but with yellow wash to underparts and brown iris.

ⓔ ❹ Yellow Warbler   *Dendroica petechia*   Canario María

Length: 12 cm

Common resident; near-endemic race *aureola* (also occurs on the Cocos Islands). Breeds on all the islands and found in all habitats, nesting during the warm/wet season from December to May.

IDENTIFICATION: Unmistakable; the only bright yellow passerine in Galápagos. ADULT MALE: Upperparts olive-green, with some yellow edgings on darker wings and tail; face and underparts golden-yellow, with faint chestnut streaking on breast and flanks. Crown has reddish-brown patch, variable in size. ADULT FEMALE: Lacks the crown patch of male, and has olive head and upperparts, grey breast and pale yellow belly. JUVENILE: Generally greyer than female but with traces of yellow in plumage.

VOICE: A series of clear, high-pitched "*swee–swee–swee*" notes, followed by a brief staccato warbling.

BEHAVIOUR: Feeds on insects, caught by hawking like a flycatcher or by picking them off the ground.

PLATE 32

1 **Cedar Waxwing**   *Bombycilla cedrorum*   Miracielito

Length: 18 cm   Vagrant; very few records.

IDENTIFICATION: Unmistakable due to combination of black mask and prominent brown crest. Plumage sleek brown overall, darker on the wings and shading to yellow on belly and white on undertail-coverts. Tail has broad yellow tip and secondaries have red wax-like tips, usually concealed.

VOICE: A thin, high-pitched "*tseee*".

2 **Summer Tanager**   *Piranga rubra*   Cardenal Migratorio

Length: 20 cm   Vagrant; very few authenticated records. Other tanagers have been recorded but were not specifically identified; these are most likely to have been this species which breeds in North America and winters as far south as north-west South America.

IDENTIFICATION: ADULT MALE: Unmistakable; bright red overall, with a stout pale bill and beady black eye. ADULT FEMALE/IMMATURE: Olive-grey above, orange-yellow below.

VOICE: Call is a sharp, rattling "*chi–pi–tuck*", with the emphasis on the last syllable.

3 **Rose-breasted Grosbeak**   *Pheuticus ludovicianus*   Picogordio Degollado

Length: 20 cm   Vagrant; very few records.

IDENTIFICATION: A large, chunky finch with a very big, triangular bill. ADULT MALE: Head, back and tail black; belly, rump and wing-bars white; diagnostic rose-red triangle on the breast. In flight, red underwing is conspicuous. ADULT FEMALE/IMMATURE: Dark brown above, buff below, with heavy, dark streaking on mantle and underparts, narrow white crown-stripes and wing-bars, and, in flight, yellow underwing.

4 **Indigo Bunting**   *Passerina cyanea*   Azulillo

Length: 14 cm   Vagrant; only recorded once.

IDENTIFICATION: A typical bunting in shape, with thick, seed-eating bill and rather broad, slightly forked tail. ADULT MALE: Brilliant turquoise blue overall in full sunlight, but can appear black in poor light or at a distance. ADULT FEMALE: Dull brown above, paler beneath, with faint streaking on the breast. IMMATURE/NON-BREEDING MALE: Generally dark brown with blue tinges.

5 **Bobolink**   *Dolichonyx oryzivorus*   Tordo Arrocero

Length: 18 cm   Regular migrant, mainly from October to December, found chiefly in cultivated areas. Recent records from San Cristóbal indicate that the species may be resident there and could be breeding.

IDENTIFICATION: A large chunky passerine with distinctive pointed tail feathers and a conical, pointed bill. ADULT MALE: Head, underparts, wings and tail black; scapulars and rump white; hindneck buff. FEMALE/ JUVENILE: Buff-brown overall, with darker streaking on back, rump and (female only) on flanks. Head striped dark brown on sides of crown and behind eye.

VOICE: Flight call is repeated "*link*".

PLATE 33

E **1** Chatham (or San Cristóbal) Mockingbird   *Nesomimus melanotis*

Cucuve de San Cristóbal

Length: 25 cm

Uncommon resident on San Cristóbal, breeding from October to April and nesting in trees or cacti. Range does not overlap with any other species of mockingbird.

IDENTIFICATION: Similar in size and structure to Galápagos Mockingbird but intermediate in plumage between that species and Hood Mockingbird. Shows a narrow white collar, prominent streaking on flanks and sides of breast, which often extends to form a diffuse breast-band, and a distinct dark malar stripe. Iris greenish.

VOICE: Loud and melodious but variable.

E **2** Charles (or Floreana) Mockingbird   *Nesomimus trifasciatus*

Cucuve de Floreana

Length: 28 cm

Rare resident, now confined to the islets of Champion-by-Floreana and Gardner-by-Floreana where the population is estimated to be around 150 birds. Conservation status: **ENDANGERED**. Range does not overlap with any other species of mockingbird. Little information is available on the species' breeding biology, although it is known to nest on Prickly Pear *Opuntia* cacti.

IDENTIFICATION: Similar to Galápagos Mockingbird but bill slightly longer and plumage shows extensive dark smudging on flanks and less streaked upperparts. Lacks the dark ear-coverts and white collar of the other mockingbird species. Iris red-brown.

VOICE: Loud and melodious but variable.

E **3** Galápagos Mockingbird   *Nesomimus parvulus*   Cucuve de Galápagos

Length: 25 cm

Locally common resident, breeding from October to April and nesting in trees or cacti. Range does not overlap with any other species of mockingbird. Six subspecies are recognised: *barringtoni* (Santa Fé); *bauri* (Genovesa); *hulli* (Darwin); *parvulus* (Fernandina, Isabela, Santa Cruz, Seymour and Daphne); *personatus* (Pinta, Marchena, Santiago and Rábida) and *wenmani* (Wolf).

IDENTIFICATION: A medium-sized, streaked landbird with long tail, short wings and narrow, moderately long, decurved bill. Upperparts dark grey-brown; wings dark brown with feathers edged and tipped white. Tail dark with white tip. Underparts white, extending up side of neck to form a broad collar; some streaking on flanks and side of breast. Does not generally show a distinct malar stripe. White supercilium contrasts with crown and dark ear-coverts. Iris colour varies from reddish-brown to yellowish-green.

VOICE: Loud and melodious but variable.

E **4** Hood Mockingbird   *Nesomimus macdonaldi*   Cucuve de Española

Length: 28 cm

Common resident on Española and Gardner-by-Española, breeding from March to April and nesting in trees or cacti. Range does not overlap with any other species of mockingbird.

IDENTIFICATION: The largest of the mockingbirds in Galápagos with the longest and heaviest bill, and the longest legs. Plumage similar to Galápagos Mockingbird but has a narrower and less conspicuous white collar, and shows heavier streaking on flanks and sides of breast which often extends to form a diffuse, mottled breast-band. Prominent dark malar stripe. Iris hazel.

VOICE: Similar to other species of mockingbird but more strident.

BEHAVIOUR: Travels mainly on foot and rarely flies. Often found in flocks outside the breeding season. Can be extremely tame.

PLATE 34

Identification of Darwin's Finches

The 13 species of Darwin's finch that occur on Galápagos pose by far the greatest identification challenge. Although some of the species are readily identified, it is often extremely difficult to separate others with confidence. This is mainly due to the similarity between some of the species and the variation between different populations of the same species. To confuse matters even more, hybrids also occur. It is therefore often impossible to identify every bird seen and confusing individuals are best left unnamed. However, the distribution of the species is reasonably well understood and, although not strictly scientific, it helps in the identification process to be aware that not all the species occur on all the islands! The checklist of species on pages 150–154 includes a summary of the distribution of the finches.

The species fall into three genera: *Geospiza* (ground finches – 4 species, and cactus finches – 2 species); *Camarhynchus* (Vegetarian Finch, tree finches – 3 species, and Woodpecker and Mangrove Finches); and *Certhidea* (Warbler Finch). However, in terms of plumage features the species are best divided into three groups:

- ground finches and cactus finches (adult males are entirely black);
- Vegetarian Finch and tree finches (adult males have black heads and olive or brown streaked bodies); and
- Woodpecker, Mangrove and Warbler Finch (males and females are alike, being mainly brown or grey).

Although there are differences in plumage and structure between these groups and, in some cases, between the species within each group, the key to identification is the shape, structure and relative size of the bill. Photographs of all of the species appear on Plates 35–38, and a description of the main identification features is included in the accompanying text. However, it is not possible to compare directly the bills of each of the species on these plates and the aim of this section is to highlight the key differences between the species in a form that allows direct comparison. The illustrations opposite are based on measured drawings of a typical bill for each species (indicated by a yellow line) overlaid on a photograph.

Ground finches (4 species) – PLATE 35 and cactus finches (2 species) – PLATE 36

PLUMAGE: ADULT MALES: Black with white-tipped undertail-coverts (except in Sharp-beaked Ground Finch where the undertail-coverts are rufous); adult plumage acquired gradually through a sequence of five moults, the black feathering appearing first on the back and subsequently on the throat, breast and belly. Bill pale pinkish or yellowish, becoming black during the breeding season. FEMALES/IMMATURES: Brown with variable amounts of streaking; generally palest on the underparts.

BILL SIZE, SHAPE AND STRUCTURE: Distinguished as a group from the other types of finch by their rather conical bills with a relatively straight bottom edge to the lower mandible. The bills of cactus finches are similar but are more elongated and pointed and generally appear slightly decurved.

Vegetarian Finch (1 species) and tree finches (3 species)– PLATE 37

PLUMAGE: ADULT MALES: Black head (and neck, breast and back in Vegetarian Finch) when mature, the remainder of the plumage being olive-brown with some dark streaking (the belly of Vegetarian Finch is white). Bill pale pinkish or yellowish, becoming black during the breeding season. FEMALES/IMMATURES: Olive-brown with faint streaking; less heavily streaked on the underparts than ground or cactus finches.

BILL SIZE, SHAPE AND STRUCTURE: Distinguished as a group from the other types of finch as both the culmen and the bottom edge of the lower mandible are curved, giving the bill a rather parrot-like appearance.

Woodpecker, Mangrove and Warbler Finches (3 species) – PLATE 38

PLUMAGE: ADULT MALES AND FEMALES/IMMATURES: Sexes alike. Uniform and virtually unstreaked olive, greyish, buff or brown. Bill pale pinkish or yellowish, becoming black during the breeding season.

BILL SIZE, SHAPE AND STRUCTURE: Woodpecker and Mangrove Finches are distinguished from the other types of finch by their rather stout, long and pointed bills with curved culmen. Warbler Finch is distinguished by its small, thin, pointed bill which is very similar to that of a warbler.

Deeper at base than length of upper mandible; base of upper mandible typically starts on forehead and forms raised ridge. Culmen sharply curved but bottom edge to the lower mandible relatively straight.

LARGE GROUND FINCH

Very variable but length of upper mandible always greater than depth of bill at base, and bill never as dainty or pointed as that of Small Ground Finch. Culmen curved but bottom edge to the lower mandible relatively straight.

MEDIUM GROUND FINCH

Dainty and rather pointed, the culmen being slightly curved and bottom edge to the lower mandible being relatively straight.

SMALL GROUND FINCH

Small and distinctly pointed, proportionately longer and thinner than any of the other ground finches with a straighter culmen and bottom edge to the lower mandible.

SHARP-BEAKED GROUND FINCH

Rather stout, but long and pointed with a distinctly curved culmen – similar to that of a tanager.

WOODPECKER FINCH

Similar to Woodpecker Finch but shorter and less heavy.

MANGROVE FINCH

Small, thin, pointed and slightly decurved, very similar to that of a warbler.

WARBLER FINCH

Subspecies *conirostris* (from Española): heavy and similar to Large Ground Finch but laterally compressed and more elongated and pointed than that species; the upper mandible is always longer than the depth of the bill at base.

LARGE CACTUS FINCH

Subspecies *propinqua* (from Genovesa): similar to that of *conirostris* but smaller, narrower and more pointed (subspecies *darwini* from Darwin and Wolf is similar).

LARGE CACTUS FINCH

Rather distinctive: relatively thick but distinctly elongated and slightly decurved. The culmen is slightly curved and the bottom edge to the lower mandible is relatively straight.

CACTUS FINCH

Relatively short, deep at the base and broad, with distinctly curved culmen and curved bottom edge to lower mandible.

VEGETARIAN FINCH

Moderately long and stout, and distinctly parrot-like; the culmen is sharply curved, mirrored by an upward curve to the bottom edge of the lower mandible. The tips of the mandibles generally cross, a diagnostic characteristic of this species.

LARGE TREE FINCH

Similar to, but not as parrot-like as, Large Tree Finch, being less stout and with a less sharply curved culmen; the tips of the mandibles do not cross.

MEDIUM TREE FINCH

Relatively small and rather stubby, both the culmen and the bottom edge of the lower mandible being noticeably curved.

SMALL TREE FINCH

PLATE 35

E **①** **Large Ground Finch** *Geospiza magnirostris* Pinzón Grande de Tierra

Length: 16 cm

Uncommon resident, least numerous on islands where Medium Ground Finch occurs. Occurs in the arid zone where it is usually found singly; does not feed in flocks. Feeds on the ground less often than the other ground finches. Breeds mainly during the warm/wet season.

IDENTIFICATION: The largest of the ground finches with a massive bill, the depth at the base being equal to the length of the upper mandible. The base of the upper mandible often begins on the forehead and forms a raised ridge (SEE PAGE 101). ADULT MALE: Wholly black with white-tipped undertail-coverts. FEMALE/IMMATURE: Brown with streaked underparts.

VOICE: A rather slow, low-pitched but distinctive song: "*teu–e–e–e– …leur*" or "*teu–woo–whu*".

E **②** **Small Ground Finch** *Geospiza fuliginosa* Pinzón Pequeno de Tierra

Length: 11 cm

Abundant and widespread resident. Most numerous in the coastal, arid and transition zones, breeding during the warm/wet season and moving into the highlands at other times of the year. Often forms a symbiotic relationship with Giant Tortoises and Marine and Land Iguanas, feeding on skin parasites.

IDENTIFICATION: The smallest, most compact ground finch with a rather dainty, short, pointed bill, the culmen being slightly curved (SEE PAGE 101). ADULT MALE: Wholly black with white-tipped undertail-coverts. FEMALE/IMMATURE: Brown with streaked underparts.

VOICE: A rather weak but rapid disyllabic song: "*twichooo–twichooo*" or "*teur–weee*".

E **③** **Medium Ground Finch** *Geospiza fortis* Pinzón Mediano de Tierra

Length: 12·5 cm

Abundant and widespread resident. Most numerous in the coastal, arid and transition zones, often forming mixed flocks with Small Ground Finches. Breeds mainly during the warm/wet season, often moving to the highlands outside this period.

IDENTIFICATION: Intermediate between Small and Large Ground Finch in size. Whilst the size of the bill is very variable, it is never as dainty or as pointed as Small Ground and, unlike in Large Ground, the length of the upper mandible is always greater than the depth of the bill (SEE PAGE 101). ADULT MALE: Wholly black with white-tipped undertail-coverts. FEMALE/IMMATURE: Brown with streaked underparts.

VOICE: Song similar to but slightly louder than Small Ground, often with trisyllabic notes: "*teur–weee–wee*" or "*tee–er–loo*".

E **④** **Sharp-beaked Ground Finch** *Geospiza difficilis* Pinzón Vampiro

Length: 12·5 cm

Locally common resident. Three subspecies are recognised: *debilirostris* (Fernandina and Santiago); *difficilis* (Genovesa and Pinta) and *septentrionalis* (Darwin and Wolf). Generally found in the highlands, breeding during the warm/wet season but disperses to the lowlands outside this period; confined to the shore and arid zones on Genovesa, Darwin and Wolf. The population on Wolf and Darwin is often referred to as the Vampire Finch since the birds there regularly feed on blood obtained by pecking at the base of Nazca Booby feathers.

IDENTIFICATION: Very similar to Small Ground Finch but bill longer and more pointed, the culmen being less curved (SEE PAGE 101). ADULT MALE: Wholly black with rufous undertail-coverts. FEMALE/IMMATURE: Generally darker than the other species of ground finch.

VOICE: A rather feeble song with short notes, reminiscent of Warbler Finch (Plate 38).

PLATE 36

E **①** **Cactus Finch** *Geospiza scandens* Pinzón del Cactus

Length: 14 cm

Locally common resident. Four subspecies are recognised: *abingdoni* (Pinta); *intermedia* (Santa Fé, Floreana, Santa Cruz, Isabela and Pinzón (although it may be extinct on this island)); *rothschildi* (Marchena); and *scandens* (Santiago and Rábida). Restricted to the arid zone and rarely seen away from areas of Prickly Pear Cacti *Opuntia*, upon which nests are built. Breeds during the warm/wet season.

IDENTIFICATION: Plumage characteristics similar to the ground finches but bill rather distinctive, being long and pointed and appearing slightly decurved (SEE PAGE 101). ADULT MALE: Wholly black with white-tipped undertail-coverts. FEMALE/IMMATURE: Brown and heavily streaked, particularly around the head and neck which often appears quite dark, a feature which distinguishes the species from the ground finches.

VOICE: Most frequent call is a loud, ringing "*teur–lee, teur–lee*", but also gives a "*teur–teur–teur–twee*". Occasionally sings in flight.

E **②** **Large Cactus Finch** *Geospiza conirostris* Pinzón Grande de Cactus

Length: 15 cm

Locally common resident. Three subspecies are recognised: *conirostris* **2A** (Española); *darwinii* (Darwin and Wolf); and *propinqua* **2B** (Genovesa). Does not occur on islands where Cactus Finch is present. Breeds during the warm/wet season. Often feeds on the ground.

IDENTIFICATION: Plumage characteristics similar to the ground finches and Cactus Finch. ADULT MALE: Wholly black with white-tipped undertail-coverts. FEMALE/IMMATURE: Dull black or dark grey, often with faint white fringes to the feathers on the underparts; the darkest of all the ground and cactus finches.

Subspecies *conirostris* **2A** is slightly larger than *propinqua* **2B** and darwinii, with a heavier bill which is similar to Large Ground Finch but laterally compressed and more elongated and pointed; the upper mandible is always longer than the depth of the bill at base. Bills of *propinqua* and *darwinii* are smaller, narrower and more pointed (SEE PAGE 101).

VOICE: A rather distinctive "*chee–yoo–oo*" or "*klee–yoo*".

PLATE 37

E ❶ Vegetarian Finch *Camarhynchus crassirostris* Pinzón Vegetariano

Length: 16 cm

Uncommon resident; generally found in the transition zone but occasionally in the arid and humid zones. Breeds principally during the warm/wet season. Has a distinctly upright stance when perched, feeding quietly and moving rather slowly.

IDENTIFICATION: Distinguished by large size and short, broad bill which is deep at the base (SEE PAGE 101). ADULT MALE: Head, neck, breast and back black when fully mature, the remainder of the plumage being olive-brown and streaked, apart from the belly which is white. Bill pale pinkish or yellowish becoming black during the breeding season. FEMALE/IMMATURE: Upperparts brown and streaked, with unstreaked olive rump. Underparts pale, whitish or yellowish, with dark streaks on breast and flanks.

VOICE: A rather loud and distinctive song which comprises several musical notes followed by a harsh buzz and often ending with a lower-pitched whistle.

E ❷ Large Tree Finch *Camarhynchus psittacula* Pinzón Grande de Árbol

Length: 13 cm

Uncommon resident. Three subspecies are recognised: *affinis* (Isabela, Fernandina); *habeli* (Pinta, Marchena); and *psittacula* (Seymour, Santa Fé, Santa Cruz, Floreana, Pinzón, Rábida, Santiago and possibly San Cristóbal). Breeds in the highlands, mainly during the warm/wet season, often moving to lower elevations at other times.

IDENTIFICATION: The largest of the tree finches with a large, rather parrot-like bill, the tips of the mandibles crossing (SEE PAGE 101). ADULT MALE: Head, neck, breast and mantle black when fully mature, the remainder of the upperparts being olive-grey with some dark streaking (however, commonest plumage has black restricted to head and throat). Underparts pale, often with a yellow tinge, but with dark streaks, particularly on upper breast. FEMALE/IMMATURE: Upperparts olive-brown with faint streaking. Underparts paler and virtually unstreaked, sometimes with a yellowish wash.

VOICE: A rather soft, low-pitched song that typically includes a ringing and often repeated "*toorelu*" or "*twee–twee*" and generally ends with a series of high-pitched "*e*" notes.

E ❸ Medium Tree Finch *Camarhynchus pauper* Pinzón Mediano de Árbol

Length: 13 cm

Fairly common resident, restricted to Floreana where most numerous in the highlands, sometimes moving to lower elevations outside the breeding season. Breeds when conditions are suitable, principally during the warm/wet season. Conservation Status: NEAR-THREATENED.

IDENTIFICATION: Similar in size to Large Tree Finch but bill smaller and less parrot-like (the tips of the mandibles do not cross) (SEE PAGE 101). Respective plumages similar to those of Large Tree Finch.

VOICE: Virtually indistinguishable from Large Tree Finch but sometimes gives a five-syllable "*tshoo–tshoo–tshoo–tshoo–tshoo*" and occasionally a "*tsee–tsee–tsee*".

E ❹ Small Tree Finch *Camarhynchus parvulus* Pinzón Pequeño de Árbol

Length: 11 cm

Common and widespread resident. Two subspecies are recognised: *parvulus* (Santiago, Rábida, Santa Cruz, Seymour, Santa Fé, Isabela, Pinzón, Floreana and Fernandina); and *salvini* (San Cristóbal). Most numerous in the highlands but also occurs in the arid zone, particularly outside the breeding season. Breeds principally during the warm/wet season. Often feeds upside-down at the end of branches, reminiscent of a chickadee or tit. Occasionally feeds on the ground.

IDENTIFICATION: The smallest of the tree finches with a small, rather stubby bill (SEE PAGE 101). ADULT MALE: Plumage similar to the other tree finches but underparts generally pale yellow with restricted amount of streaking on upper breast. FEMALE/IMMATURE: Upperparts grey-brown with very faint streaking. Underparts paler and virtually unstreaked. Often has a pale area around eye and a hint of a pale supercilium.

VOICE: Very variable, virtually indistinguishable from other tree finches.

PLATE 38

E **①** **Woodpecker Finch** *Camarhynchus pallidus* Pinzón Artesano

Length: 15 cm

Locally common resident. Three subspecies are recognised: *pallidus* (Santiago, Rábida, Pinzón, Santa Cruz and Seymour) **1A**; *productus* (Fernandina and Isabela) **1B**; and *striatipectus* (San Cristóbal). Most numerous in the highlands, although also present and breeds in the lowlands, nesting whenever conditions are suitable. Distinctive behaviour whilst searching for food, often looking and probing under branches, leaves or rocks in a manner reminiscent of a nuthatch. One of the few species of bird in the world that uses a tool, some individuals having learned to manipulate a twig or thorn in its bill to ease insects out of crevices.

IDENTIFICATION: Males and females are alike. Upperparts uniform and virtually unstreaked olive or brown; underparts yellowish or whitish, usually unstreaked but sometimes with fine grey streaking on upper breast. Bill long and rather stout with a distinctly curved culmen, similar to that of a tanager (SEE PAGE 101).

VOICE: A rapid, loud and distinctive song which comprises seven or eight notes followed by a prolonged "seee". Also occasionally gives other calls, such as a loud "*cheer—keee–e–e–e*" or "*tchurr–tchurr–tchur–e–e–e*".

E **②** **Mangrove Finch** *Camarhynchus heliobates* Pinzón del Manglar

Length: 14 cm

Very rare resident, confined to dense stands of mangrove on the west coast of Isabela and possibly the east coast of Fernandina. The population must be very small, due to the restricted range of its favoured habitat, and may number no more than a few dozen birds. Conservation Status: **CRITICALLY ENDANGERED**. Some birds occasionally use a twig to ease insects out of crevices, using the same technique as the Woodpecker Finch.

IDENTIFICATION: Males and females are alike. Similar to Woodpecker Finch but slightly smaller, with a less heavy bill and generally greyer plumage which does not show yellowish tinges. The upperparts are grey-brown with a slight olive hue to the rump, and the underparts are greyish-white with some grey spotting on breast. Often shows a distinctive pale area around eye (SEE PAGE 101).

VOICE: A rather loud and distinctive song which comprises two or three syllables, usually repeated three times: typically "*ds–shed–ee, ds–shed–ee, ds–shed–ee*", occasionally ending with a rising, prolonged "*tseee*".

E **③** **Warbler Finch** *Certhidia olivacea* Pinzón Cantor

Length: 10 cm

Common and widespread resident; found in all vegetation zones, being most numerous in the humid zone although common in the arid zone on the smaller islands. Breeds whenever conditions are suitable, principally during the warm/wet season. Eight subspecies are recognised: *becki* (Darwin and Wolf); *bifasciata* (Santa Fé); *cinerascens* (Española) **3A**; *fusca* (Marchena and Pinta); *luteola* (San Cristóbal); *mentalis* (Genovesa) **3B**; *olivacea* (Fernandina, Isabela, Pinzón, Rábida, Santa Cruz, Santiago and Seymour) **3C**; and *ridgwayi* (Floreana).

IDENTIFICATION: By far the smallest of the Darwin's finches, with the smallest, narrowest bill which is very similar to that of a warbler. The plumage of the different subspecies vary: the colour of the upperparts ranges from pale grey to olive-green, and the underparts from white to buff. Some subspecies show a distinct pale eye-ring. Whilst males and females generally have identical plumage, some adult males (particularly of subspecies olivacea) develop an orange throat-patch. The lack of yellow in the plumage distinguishes the Warbler Finch from the slightly larger Yellow Warbler (see plate 31), which is the only likely confusion species (SEE PAGE 101).

VOICE: A rather feeble but melodious warbling song, usually ending with a high-pitched buzz.

THE REPTILES OF GALÁPAGOS

Introduction

Twenty eight species of reptile have been recorded in Galápagos in recent times. Nineteen of these species are endemic to the archipelago, 11 of which are confined to single islands, and three species have been introduced. There is also possibly an undescribed species of Leaf-toed Gecko on Rábida. The reptiles that occur in Galápagos can be divided into seven 'types'. These are shown in the following table which indicates the number of species recorded and provides a summary of their status.

Type (Plate No.)	Species Recorded	Status			Endemic Species
		Indigenous Residents	Marine Migrants	Introduced	
Tortoise (39)	1	1			1
Turtles (40)	4	1	3		
Iguanas (41)	3	3			3
Lava lizards (42)	7	7			7
Geckos (43)	9 (10?)	6 (7?)		3	5 (6?)
Snakes (44)	3	3			3
Sea snakes (44)	1		1		

The types of reptile

This part of the book provides an introduction to each of the seven 'types' of reptile that occur in Galápagos. It aims to aid initial identification, and the text for each of the groups is cross-referenced to the relevant plate(s) that follow.

Galápagos Tortoise

TORTOISES   Family: **Testudinidae**
1 species recorded   **(Plate 39)**
(indigenous resident), represented by 11 subspecies

Endemic species: Galápagos (or Giant) Tortoise.

Tortoises are unmistakable reptiles, readily distinguished by their hard, dome-shaped carapace which is formed of bony plates which are fused to the skeleton. They differ from the turtles in being entirely terrestrial, their legs being adapted for walking rather than swimming. The Galápagos Tortoise grows to a very large size (sometimes up to 250 kg) and exhibits two distinct carapace types: dome-shaped and 'saddleback', the latter having a raised ridge at the front edge.

Black Turtle

TURTLES — Family: Cheloniidae

4 species recorded (Plate 40)
(1 indigenous resident; 3 marine migrants)

Turtles are unmistakable reptiles. They are almost entirely marine, only coming ashore to lay their eggs. They have hard, rather flattened carapaces which, as with the tortoises, are formed of fused bony plates. They differ from tortoises in having legs which are flattened to form flippers.

Marine Iguana (male)

IGUANAS — Family: Iguanidae

3 species recorded (Plate 41)
(all indigenous residents), one represented by 7 subspecies

Endemic species: LAND IGUANA; MARINE IGUANA; SANTA FÉ LAND IGUANA.

Iguanas are medium-sized to largish reptiles with long, tapering tails, rather stout bodies and broad heads. They are distinguished from lizards by their larger size, the presence of a row of spines along the back (particularly prominent in males) and rather broad heads.

LAVA LIZARDS — Family: Iguanidae

7 species recorded (Plate 42)
(all indigenous residents)

Endemic species: ESPAÑOLA LAVA LIZARD; FLOREANA LAVA LIZARD; GALÁPAGOS LAVA LIZARD; MARCHENA LAVA LIZARD; PINTA LAVA LIZARD; PINZÓN LAVA LIZARD; SAN CRISTÓBAL LAVA LIZARD.

Lava lizards are small reptiles with long, tapering tails, slim bodies and rather pointed heads. Their toes are long and pointed, quite different from those of the geckos which are the only likely confusion species. The average size of the species varies between islands and the markings are extremely variable even within the same species. Unlike geckos, they are active during the day.

Galápagos Lava Lizard (male)

Galápagos Leaf-toed Gecko

GECKOS
Family: Gekkonidae
10 species recorded **(Plate 43)**
(7 indigenous residents, one of which may now be extinct; 3 introduced)

Endemic species: BAUR'S LEAF-TOED GECKO; GALÁPAGOS LEAF-TOED GECKO; RÁBIDA LEAF-TOED GECKO (undescribed, possibly **EXTINCT**); SAN CRISTÓBAL LEAF-TOED GECKO; SANTA FÉ LEAF-TOED GECKO; WENMAN LEAF-TOED GECKO.

Geckos are very small, nocturnally-active reptiles. They resemble lava lizards but have thicker tails and rather broad heads with large eyes. Their toes are diagnostic, having folds of skin which form pads enabling them to climb even smooth vertical surfaces with ease.

Española Snake

SNAKES
Family: Colubridae
3 species recorded (3 terrestrial indigenous residents, two of which **(Plate 44)** are represented by 3 subspecies and the other by 2 subspecies)

Endemic species: FLOREANA SNAKE (includes named subspecies Española Snake and San Cristóbal Snake); GALÁPAGOS SNAKE (includes named subspecies Fernandina Snake and Isabela Snake); SLEVIN'S SNAKE (includes named subspecies Steindachner's Snake).

Snakes are unmistakable reptiles, readily distinguished from all others by their long, thin bodies and the absence of legs.

Yellow-bellied Sea Snake

SEA SNAKES
Family: Hydrophiidae
1 species recorded **(Plate 44)**
(migrant marine species)

Similar in structure to the terrestrial snakes but the only species recorded in Galápagos, the Yellow-bellied (or Pelagic) Sea Snake, is entirely marine. It is characterised by its black and yellow pattern and flattened tail, an adaptation for swimming.

The reptile plates

The species illustrated All the species of tortoise, turtle, iguana and snake to have been recorded in Galápagos are illustrated in the following plates. Due to the great similarity between the species of lava lizard and gecko, and since most of the species are found only on single islands where they are the only representative of their group, a few examples only are illustrated. However, all species are covered in the text facing the plates.

The species order For ease of reference, the plates are ordered so that all the potential confusion species are grouped together. The text follows the sequence in which the species appear on the plate, from top to bottom. The species are numbered sequentially and the following annotations are used on the plates:

1 Adult (species 1)
1m Male
1f Female
1i Immature

Distribution maps A distribution map accompanies the text for each of the resident species or, in some cases, types of reptile. As with the maps used in the bird section, three 'groups' of islands have been moved to save space (see page 33 for further details). The distribution of the species is shown as solid colour on the maps in this section, as in the 'dummy' map opposite.

English name The English names used in this book for the reptiles are those most commonly cited in recent literature.

Spanish name The Spanish names shown are those which are most regularly used in Galápagos.

Endemic species The names of species which are endemic to Galápagos are preceded by an **E**.

Status The first part of the text for each species provides information on its status. This includes details of whether it is an indigenous resident, a migrant/vagrant or an introduced species, and provides a summary of its breeding season(s) and habitat preferences. The names of endemic subspecies are given in this section where appropriate.

Measurements The maximum recorded length of each species is given.

Identification Details of the features which are key to the identification of the species are given, differences between males and females being described where appropriate. Some species are virtually impossible to identify unless examined in the hand which is not permitted under the Galápagos National Park rules without a special scientific permit.

Behaviour Particular behavioural characteristics which help in the identification of a species are highlighted where appropriate.

Breeding range (regular)
· Breeding site
Regularly seen at sea
Occasionally seen at sea
Rarely seen at sea

PLATE 39

● Galápagos (or Giant) Tortoise *Geochelone elephantopus* Galápago

Length: up to 150 cm over the curve of the carapace, with different subspecies growing to different sizes. Weight: up to 250 kg

Locally common, found mainly in the highlands but often descending to lower elevations during the warm/wet season. Endemic to Galápagos; fourteen subspecies have been described, although only 11 of these still survive: abindgoni (Pinta – now **EXTINCT** in the wild); becki (Volcán Wolf, Isabela); chathamensis (San Cristóbal); darwini (Santiago); elephantopus (Cerro Azul, Isabela); ephippium (Pinzón); guntheri (Sierra Negra, Isabela); hoodensis (Española) ●A; microphyes (Volcán Darwin, Isabela); porteri (Santa Cruz) ●I; and vandenburghi (Volcán Alcedo, Isabela). The total population is estimated to number c.15,000.

IDENTIFICATION: Unmistakable due to its large size and distinctive shape. The Galápagos Tortoise exhibits two distinct carapace shapes: dome-shelled and saddle-backed, although intermediate forms do occur. The dome-shelled subspecies (*chathamensis, elephantopus, guntheri, porteri* ●I and *vandenburghi*) generally have shorter legs and necks than the saddle-backed subspecies (*abindgoni, ephippium* and *hoodensis* ●A), in which the front edge of the carapace is raised enabling maximum elevation of the long neck. The carapace in saddlebacks is usually narrowed at the rear end and these subspecies also have much longer legs than dome-shelled forms. The carapace of subspecies *microphyes* and *darwini* are intermediate in shape, being rather flattened, although they are not elevated at the front. The carapace shape of subspecies *becki* is very variable, some individuals being dome-shaped, others flattened, and others distinctly saddleback-shaped.

In all subspecies the sexes are alike, although males are much larger than females, and have a concave plastron (ventral plate) and a noticeably longer and thicker tail.

VOICE: Usually silent but during copulation males emit a loud, deep groan which can be heard over a considerable distance.

BEHAVIOUR: Tortoises are usually only active from about 08.00 until 16.00. Mating may occur in almost any month of the year but reaches a peak during the warm/wet season, with eggs usually hatching between December and April. Sexual maturity is attained at the age of about 20–25 years. During the breeding season males chase each other and posture by raising their heads as high as possible, the dominant individuals being those able to raise their heads the highest.

GALÁPAGOS TORTOISE SUBSPECIES

- Ⓐ hoodensis
- Ⓑ abindgoni
- Ⓒ ephippium
- Ⓓ becki
- Ⓔ darwini
- Ⓕ microphyes
- Ⓖ elephantopus
- Ⓗ guntheri
- Ⓘ porteri
- Ⓙ chathamensis
- Ⓚ vandenburghi

PLATE 40

1 **Leatherback Turtle**   *Dermochelys coriacea*   Tortuga Land

Length: up to 188 cm   Occasional migrant; only ever seen alive at sea in Galápagos.

IDENTIFICATION: The largest turtle in the world and highly distinctive. The carapace is tapered towards the rear and is black with pale spots covered by leathery skin which forms 7 ridges that run along its entire length. The head lacks scales and is rounded, although there is a tooth-like projection on the upper mandible.

2 **Olive Ridley Turtle**   *Lepidochelys olivacea*   Tortuga Golfina

Length: up to 76 cm   Occasional migrant; only ever seen alive at sea in Galápagos.

IDENTIFICATION: Carapace greyish-green and rounded, with 6–9 costals (the outermost large plates) which are unequal in shape. The vertebral scutes (central plates) are small and also unequal in shape. The head is quite broad and has a distinctly hooked beak.

3 **Hawksbill Turtle**   *Eretmochelys imbricata*   Tortuga Carey

Length: up to 90 cm   Occasional migrant; only ever seen alive at sea in Galápagos.

IDENTIFICATION: Carapace dark brown, often with tortoiseshell markings, and teardrop-shaped, tapering towards the rear, with a slight keel. The vertebral scutes (central plates) overlap and have diagnostic 'W'-shaped rear margins (although this can sometime be difficult to see). The head is rather pointed with a prominent, hooked beak.

4 **Black (or Pacific Green) Turtle**   *Chelonia mydas*   Tortuga Negra

Length: up to 84 cm   Locally common resident; the subspecies that occurs in Galápagos is the eastern Pacific form *agassizi* which some authorities treat as a distinct species.

IDENTIFICATION: Carapace blackish to olive-brown and teardrop-shaped, tapering towards the rear, with a slight keel. The vertebral scutes (central plates) are roughly equal in size and are hexagonal with straight edges; they are about the same size as the costals (the outermost large plates). The head is rounded and the beak is, at most, only slightly hooked. The sexes are alike, although females are distinctly larger than males, and males have a concave plastron.

BEHAVIOUR: Almost entirely marine, coming ashore usually only to lay eggs. Egg-laying takes place from December to June, with a peak in activity during February. Egg-laying usually takes place at night.

PLATE 41

Marine Iguana *Amblyrhynchus cristatus* Iguana Marina

Length: 60–150 cm, different subspecies growing to different sizes: individuals on Isabela, Santa Cruz and Fernandina are the largest and those on Genovesa and Española the smallest. (Hatchlings are similar in size to lava lizards.)

Abundant in the shore zone on all the islands. Seven subspecies are recognised: *albemarlensis* (Isabela) **1D**; *cristatus* (Fernandina) **1A**; *hassi* (Santa Cruz) **1B**; *mertensi* (San Cristóbal and Santiago); *nanus* (Genovesa); *sielmanni* (Pinta); and *venustissimus* (Española and Gardner-near-Española) **1C**. The total population is estimated to number *c.* 250,000. Hybrids with Land Iguana have been recorded on South Plaza.

IDENTIFICATION: Large and dark with variable coloration. Distinguished from the land iguanas by the flattened, rather square nose, an adaptation for feeding on marine algae, and by the laterally flattened tail, an adaptation for swimming. ADULT MALE: Row of long spines on head and along back and tail. Variable pattern on body which ranges from red and black (*venustissimus* on Española), through green, yellow and black (e.g. *albemarlensis* on Isabela) to predominantly dark sooty-grey (*cristatus* on Fernandina). During the mating season assumes considerably brighter coloration. ADULT FEMALE/JUVENILE: Much smaller than adult males and wholly dark, with ridge of short spines along back and tail.

BEHAVIOUR: Found predominantly along rocky shores, females or immatures often basking together in large numbers. The only marine lizard in the world, feeding on marine algae either obtained from the splash zone or by diving close to the shore; can spend up to an hour under water. Sometimes climbs trees or cacti to bask in the sun. Strongly territorial, particularly during the breeding season. Male shakes head rapidly up and down and exhales loudly when agitated. Breeds from November to December. Males take up to eight years to reach sexual maturity.

Land Iguana *Conolophus subcristatus* Iguana Terrestre

Length: up to *c.*100 cm (hatchlings are similar in size to lava lizards)

Locally fairly common, inhabiting the arid zone. Hybrids with Marine Iguana have been recorded on South Plaza but do not appear to be very long-lived.

IDENTIFICATION: Large and pale, generally yellowish-orange in colour with darker brown back. Distinguished from Marine Iguana by the rather pointed nose and from the Santa Fé Land Iguana by the more restricted row of spines along the back. ADULT MALE: Row of long spines along back of neck, with shorter spines on head and along upperback. Mature individuals assume some red coloration, particularly during the mating season. ADULT FEMALE: Considerably smaller and less brightly coloured than adult male, with shorter spines.

BEHAVIOUR: Forms small colonies although often found singly. Males are highly territorial, defending their territories against intruders by engaging in head-butting battles. Breeding begins in different months on different islands: on Isabela in January, on Fernandina in June, on Santa Cruz in September and on South Plaza in January. Males can take up to 12 years to reach sexual maturity.

Santa Fé Land Iguana *Conolophus pallidus* Iguana Terrestre Galapagueña

Length: up to *c.*120 cm (hatchlings are similar in size to lava lizards)

Fairly common; confined to Santa Fé, inhabiting the arid zone.

IDENTIFICATION: Large and generally pale, whitish to dark brown in colour, often with large dark brown blotches on back. Distinguished from Marine Iguana by the rather pointed nose and from the Land Iguana by the more extensive row of spines along the back. ADULT MALE: Row of medium-length spines along neck, back and tail. In some individuals the eyes become red. ADULT FEMALE: Considerably smaller than adult male, with shorter spines.

BEHAVIOUR: Found throughout Santa Fé away from the shoreline, forming small colonies but often found singly. Like the other iguanas, males are highly territorial, defending their territories against intruders by engaging in head-butting battles. Mating occurs in February and March. Males can take up to 12 years to reach sexual maturity.

SPECIES

██ Marine Iguana

█ Land Iguana

█ Santa Fé Land Iguana

PLATE 42

E Lava Lizards *Microlophus* (= *Tropidurus*) spp.   Lagartija de lava

Common in the shore and arid zones. Seven species occur, all of which are endemic. Six of the species are confined to single islands, as reflected by their common names:

1 **Galápagos Lava Lizard** *Microlophus albemarlensis*
(Baltra, Daphne Major, Fernandina, Isabela, North Seymour, South Plaza, Rábida, Santa Cruz, Santa Fé, and Santiago)

2 **Española Lava Lizard** *Microlophus delanonis*

3 **Floreana Lava Lizard** *Microlophus grayi*
(also occus on Caldwell, Champion, Enderby and Gardner-near-Floreana)

4 **Marchena Lava Lizard** *Microlophus habellii*

5 **Pinta Lava Lizard** *Microlophus pacificus* (not illustrated)

6 **Pinzón Lava Lizard** *Microlophus duncanensis*

7 **San Cristóbal Lava Lizard** *Microlophus bivattatus*

> Length: 15–30 cm
> Different species grow to different sizes: the largest is the **Española Lava Lizard** (up to 30 cm) and the smallest is the **Floreana Lava Lizard** (rarely more than 15 cm)

IDENTIFICATION: Lava lizards are readily identified by their relatively small size and long, tapering tails, slim bodies and rather pointed heads. The toes are long and pointed and the skin is scaly, quite different from the geckos which are the only likely confusion species. Specific identification is impossible without first catching individuals. However, the fact that no more than one species occurs on any one island does facilitate identification.

ADULT MALE: Very variable in coloration and the pattern of markings on the body. These markings are generally adapted to blend in with the substrate upon which they live. Most males are dark grey with black speckling, although some are reddish and others have pale stripes along their sides. When mature they have a black throat and develop a short crest of spiny scales which extends along the back and which can be raised during display. Males are 2–3 times heavier than females. ADULT FEMALE: Similar to male in general structure but much smaller and lacking the spiny scales along the back. When mature they have a red or orange throat which in some species (e.g. Española Lava Lizard) extends to the whole head.

BEHAVIOUR: Active during the day. Highly territorial, both males and females defending territories against intruders of the same sex. Both sexes challenge intruders initially by performing 'push-ups' with their front legs, although this behaviour is more vigorous in males. Breeding occurs from December, at the start of the warm/wet season. Males take up to three years to reach sexual maturity, whereas some females can breed when they are nine months old.

SPECIES
■ Galápagos Lava Lizard
■ Single island endemics

PLATE 43

Geckos   *Phyllodactylus* spp. and introduced species   Salamanquesa, Gecos

Locally common in the shore and arid zones and around human habitation. Ten species occur in Galápagos, six of which are endemic (although one may be extinct) and three of which have been introduced in recent times.

E **1** **Galápagos Leaf-toed Gecko** *Phyllodactylus galapagoensis* | Length: up to 15 cm
(Daphne Major, Fernandina, Isabela, Pinzón, Santa Cruz,
and Santiago); three individuals depicted, showing the highly variable coloration of this species.

E **2** **Baur's Leaf-toed Gecko** *Phyllodactylus bauri*
(Caldwell, Champion, Enderby, Española, Floreana and Gardner-near-Floreana)

E **3** **Rábida Leaf-toed Gecko** *Phyllodactylus* sp. (undescribed)
(Rábida – possibly Extinct)

E **4** **San Cristóbal Leaf-toed Gecko** *Phyllodactylus leei*
(San Cristóbal)

E **5** **Santa Fé Leaf-toed Gecko** *Phyllodactylus barringtonensis*
(Santa Fé)

6 **Tuberculated Leaf-toed Gecko** *Phyllodactylus tuberculosus*
(San Cristóbal)

E **7** **Wenman Leaf-toed Gecko** *Phyllodactylus gilberti*
(Wolf)

The three introduced species are:

8 *Gonatodes caudiscutatus*,   **9** *Lepidodactylus lugubris* and   **10** *Phyllodactylus reissi*

IDENTIFICATION: Geckos resemble lava lizards but are readily identified by their small size and rather broad heads with large, dark eyes, the pupil being a vertical slit, and permanently closed, transparent eyelids. Their toes are diagnostic, having folds of skin which form pads enabling them to climb even smooth vertical surfaces with ease. Geckos have soft skin and generally sandy- coloured bodies with dark mottling on the upper surface and often a pale line through the eye. Specific identification is impossible without first catching individuals. However, only San Cristóbal supports more than one of the indigenous species and the introduced species are restricted to areas of human habitation, principally on Santa Cruz. Identification can therefore usually be made on the basis of distribution.

BEHAVIOUR: Active only at night when they can be quite vocal, giving high-pitched squeaks. During the day they hide under rocks, logs and in cracks. Breed in October and November.

Endemic species
- Galápagos Leaf-toed Gecko **1**
- Baur's Leaf-toed Gecko **2**
- Single island endemics **3** **4** **5** **7**

Non-endemic & introduced species
- Tuberculated Leaf-toed Gecko **6**
- Introduced species **8** **9** **10**

PLATE 44

E **1** Floreana/Española/San Cristóbal Snake *Philodryas biserialis*

Length: up to 120 cm | Culebra biserialis/hoodensis/eibli

Locally fairly common. Three named subspecies occur, mainly in the arid and shore zones: Floreana Snake *biserialis* (Champion, Floreana and Gardner-near-Floreana), Española Snake *hoodensis* **1A** (Española and Gardner-near-Española) and San Cristóbal Snake *eibli* (San Cristóbal). Feeds by constricting its prey, although slightly venomous.

IDENTIFICATION: Virtually impossible to identify unless examined in the hand, identification being confirmed on the basis of the shape, pattern and number of scales on certain parts of the body. However, this species only occurs on islands from which the two other species that occur in Galápagos are absent. As with the other species, predominantly brown with yellow stripes or dark grey with yellow spots on the upperside forming a zigzag pattern.

E **2** Galápagos/Fernandina/Isabela Snake *Alsophis dorsalis*

Length: up to 120 cm | Culebra dorsalis/occidentalis/helleri

Locally fairly common. Two named subspecies occur, mainly in the arid and shore zones: Galápagos Snake *dorsalis* (Baltra, Rábida, Santa Cruz, Santa Fé and Santiago), Fernandina Snake *occidentalis* **2A** (Fernandina) and Isabela Snake helleri (Isabela and Tortuga). Feeds by constricting its prey, although slightly venomous.

IDENTIFICATION: Virtually impossible to identify unless examined in the hand, identification being confirmed on the basis of the shape, pattern and number of scales on certain parts of the body. As in the other species, predominantly brown with yellow stripes or dark grey with yellow spots on their upperside forming a zigzag pattern. However, the present species only occurs on islands from which *P. biserialis* is absent, and although present on the same islands as *A. slevini*, that species is considerably smaller.

E **3** Slevin's/Steindachner's Snake *Alsophis slevini*

Length: up to 50 cm | Culebra slevini/steindachneri

Locally fairly common. Two named subspecies occur, mainly in the arid and shore zones: Slevin's Snake *slevini* (Fernandina, Isabela and Pinzón) and Steindachner's Snake *steindachneri* **3A** (Baltra, Rábida, Santa Cruz and Santiago). Feeds by constricting its prey, although slightly venomous.

IDENTIFICATION: Virtually impossible to identify unless examined in the hand, identification being confirmed on the basis of the shape, pattern and number of scales on certain parts of the body. As in the other species, predominantly brown with yellow stripes or dark grey with yellow spots on the upperside forming a zigzag pattern. However, the present species only occurs on islands from which *P. biserialis* is absent and although present on the same islands as *A. dorsalis*, that species is considerably larger.

4 Yellow-bellied (or Pelagic) Sea Snake *Pelamis platurus* Culebra de Mar

Length: up to 85 cm | Migrant; regularly recorded at sea in Galápagos, particularly during El Niño years. Highly venomous.

IDENTIFICATION: Entirely marine. Black above and yellow below; flattened yellow tail with large black spots.

THE MAMMALS OF GALÁPAGOS

Introduction

In total, 32 indigenous species of mammal have been recorded in Galápagos in recent times. This excludes domesticated species which have become feral (dogs, cats, pigs, goats, donkeys, horses and cattle) and introduced rodents (rats and mice). Six species are endemic to the archipelago, four of which are confined to single islands. The great majority of the species recorded, 25 in total, are cetaceans (whales and dolphins). The mammals that occur in Galápagos can be divided into four 'types'. These are shown in the following table which indicates the number of species recorded and provides a summary of their status.

Type (Plate No.)	Species Recorded	Status		Endemic Species	Endemic Subspecies
		Residents	Migrants		
Sea lions (45)	2	2	1	1	
Rodents (46–47)	4	4	4		
Bats (47)	2	2		1	
Whales and dolphins (48–53)	25	25			

The types of mammal

This part of the book provides an introduction to each of the four 'types' of mammal that occur in Galápagos. It aims to aid initial identification, and the text for each of the types is cross-referenced to the relevant plate(s) that follow.

Galápagos Fur Seal

SEA LIONS   Family: Otariidae
2 species recorded (residents)   **(Plate 45)**

Endemic species: Galápagos Fur Seal

Endemic subspecies: Galápagos Sea Lion

Sea lions and fur seals are the most conspicuous mammals in Galápagos. They are unmistakable, readily distinguished by their large size, characteristic shape and webbed flippers. Seal lions and fur seals feed at sea, spending the rest of the time on land in the shore zone.

Large Fernandina Rice Rat

RODENTS   Family: Muridae
4 indigenous species recorded   **(Plates 46 and 47)**
(plus introduced rats and mice)

Endemic species: Large Fernandina Rice Rat; Santa Fé Rice Rat; Santiago Rice Rat; Small Fernandina Rice Rat

Before the arrival of man, the only species of rodent to occur in Galápagos were the rice rats. There were formerly seven species, all endemic to the archipelago, but the introduction of the ubiquitous Ship Rat is believed to have led to the extinction of three of these species. Rodents are small to medium-sized furry mammals with long scaly tails, pointed faces and short, rounded ears.

BATS — Family: Vespertilionidae
2 species recorded (indigenous residents)   (Plate 47)

Endemic subspecies: Galápagos Red Bat

Bats are unmistakable, small, furry, nocturnal, flying mammals, their wings being formed of a membrane of skin between the elongated digits of their 'hands' and their ankles.

Galápagos Red Bat

WHALES and DOLPHINS (CETACEANS)

Whales and dolphins (collectively known as cetaceans) are medium-sized to extremely large marine mammals. A total of 85 species is currently known to man and 25 of these have been reliably recorded in Galápagos.

Whilst our knowledge of the abundance, distribution and identification of cetaceans has improved tremendously since the early 1980s, there is still much to learn. Indeed, virtually nothing is known about some of the species recorded in Galápagos. This book summarises the information gathered to date on the key features for the identification of all of the cetacean species known to occur in the archipelago. Because cetacean identification is often a process of elimination, as much information as possible is given on all of the species. However, it should be borne in mind that some identification features are based on a limited number of sightings.

The information given on each species is based on our knowledge thus far, but do not be surprised if you experience something which does not fit the description in this book. Cetaceans are a constant joy to watch, not least because they are full of surprises. Just when we think it is safe to assume that Fin Whales never raise their tail flukes on diving and Pygmy Sperm Whales will not approach boats, they surprise us by doing just that! The important message here is that this section attempts to 'guide' the reader towards identification by illustrating several diagnostic features for each species – but it should not be considered definitive.

How to search for and identify cetaceans

The first challenge facing any whale watcher is finding a cetacean to identify! For this, all that is required is a pair of binoculars, a viewing platform (headland or boat) and some patience. Cetacean watching is easiest in relatively calm sea conditions, preferably with little swell and few or no white caps. Generally it is best to stand on the highest part of the platform and, if on a boat, try to look forward in front of the bow. Scan the water with the naked eye to cover the widest area and occasionally use binoculars for more distant searching. Keep searching the same area even if you think there is nothing there. Some cetaceans can dive for an hour or more.

Perhaps the most important point is to keep concentrating and remain patient. Most cetaceans are predators at the top of the food chain and, like terrestrial mammalian predators, they are not very abundant. This is all part of the excitement of whale watching, knowing that no matter how long the wait, something could pop up anywhere at any moment. Most surfacing cetaceans create their own white water so, if the sea is calm, a dark shape, a sudden splashing, or a blow is often the first sign of a sighting.

Having seen a shape in the water, the next task is to identify it. Identifying whales and dolphins at sea can be challenging for a number of reasons. The views are often brief, the animal may show little of its body above the water, and the state of the sea, weather and the sun's glare can make it difficult to establish colour, size and shape. These problems should not put off the amateur whale watcher. Whales and dolphins are magnificent and exciting creatures to watch and, like all field crafts, experience will allow the observer to identify species which seemed nearly impossible at first. However, both expert and novice must accept that because of the above difficulties, a relatively high proportion of sightings will be ascribed to one of the 'probable', 'possible' or 'haven't got a clue' categories.

The golden rule with cetacean identification is to try and pick out as many features as possible. Many species look quite similar and a number of characteristics are required for a confident identification. For example, Fin Whales can be identified by the asymmetrical coloration of the lower jaw. Unfortunately, most views at sea do not allow this feature to be noted. However, a combination of the tall straight blow, appearing before the dorsal fin as the animal surfaces, the long back, and the sloping fin combine to eliminate, with experience, the other large whales.

Having sighted a cetacean, the following features should be noted in approximate order of importance:

Size	Judging size and distance is very difficult at sea so try to compare with seabirds or boats. Remember that only part of an animal's back may be visible at any one time.
Blow	Is it visible? If so, size, shape and angle are important. Remember that the wind and the angle of the sun can affect these features.
Dorsal fin	Check its position along the back, and its size and shape.
Coloration and patterning	Colour is a variable and unreliable feature at sea and often the observer is reduced to describing coloration as 'light' or 'dark'. However, colours and, more importantly, patterns, are essential in identifying some species.
Behaviour	Behavioural traits can act as important supporting evidence for eliminating one species in favour of another. Such traits include fluking, porpoising, breaching, logging and spy-hopping.

Blow

Breaching – lifting body out of water and splashing down on surface

Spy-hopping – head lifted and held out of the water

Fluking – tail flukes raised before a dive

Cetacean features

It is helpful to have some knowledge of the structure of a cetacean and the names of the main body parts. Cetaceans also exhibit some characteristic behaviours which have specific names. Familiarity with these names will help in understanding the text on each species and will make it easier to discuss identification with other whale watchers. The terms used in this book for the various parts of a cetacean are shown on the following illustrations of Blue Whale and Striped Dolphin.

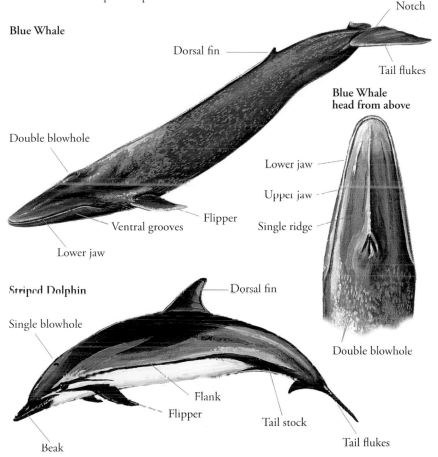

Blue Whale

Notch

Dorsal fin

Tail flukes

Blue Whale head from above

Double blowhole

Lower jaw

Upper jaw

Single ridge

Flipper

Ventral grooves

Lower jaw

Double blowhole

Striped Dolphin

Dorsal fin

Single blowhole

Flank

Flipper

Tail stock

Beak

Tail flukes

Logging – lying motionless at the surface

Porpoising – raising part or all of body clear of the water while travelling

The groups of cetacean

The cetaceans that have been recorded in Galápagos can be divided into five groups (which broadly equate to Families). This part of the book provides an introduction to each of these groups and aims to aid initial identification. It is cross-referenced to the relevant plate(s) and accompanying text which covers all of the species.

Blue Whale

RORQUAL WHALES **Family: Baleanopteridae**
6 species recorded **(Plates 48–49)**

The rorqual whales are large to very large, and include the biggest animals on earth. They differ from all other cetaceans in the region because they do not possess teeth. Instead, their upper jaws are lined with bony 'comb-like' plates called baleen which filter out small fish or zooplankton as the whale engulfs enormous quantities of seawater whilst swimming along. Rorquals have a double blowhole (single in toothed cetaceans), placed centrally on top of the head, a pleated throat capable of great expansion whilst feeding, a 'U'- to 'V'-shaped flattened head and a streamlined body for fast swimming.

Sperm Whale

SPERM WHALES **Families: Kogidae & Physeteridae**
3 species recorded **(Plates 49–50)**

Although the sperm whales include two families and the largest and smallest species of toothed whale, their basic body plans are very similar. They have a characteristic large blunt head, low underslung jaw, and a blowhole positioned to the left of the centre of the head. Sperm whales are deep divers, capable of staying below for considerable periods of time as they hunt for squid and fish.

Blainville's Beaked Whale

BEAKED WHALES **Family: Ziphidae**
3 species recorded **(Plate 50)**

These medium-sized whales live in deep water and are rarely seen at sea, making them one of the least studied mammal groups on earth. As the name suggests, they all possess a distinctive protruding beak. Their bodies are generally slim and streamlined, often with visible scarring. They have no notch in the tail and a smallish dorsal fin, positioned two-thirds of the way along the back and variable in shape. All members of the family are similar in shape and variable in colour, making identification at sea extremely difficult. The position of protruding teeth which only erupt in adult males is often the only reliable feature. If possible, any species encountered should be photographed in order to learn more of the identity and distribution of these mysterious whales.

Short-finned Pilot Whale

BLACKFISH **Family: Delphinidae**
5 species recorded **(Plate 51)**

The blackfish include the largest members of the dolphin family: the killer and pilot whales. They are predominantly black with conspicuous dorsal fins. The jaws contain many well-developed conical teeth, but the beak is small or lacking. Like other dolphins they are highly social, fast and acrobatic, often breaching, spy-hopping and lobtailing. They are extremely effective and powerful pack-hunters, able to take fish, squid, and in some cases, marine mammals.

DOLPHINS   **Family: Delphinidae**
8 species recorded   **(Plates 52–53)**

Dolphins are smaller than most whale species and possess streamlined bodies, usually with a prominent, centrally placed dorsal fin, and a protruding beak. Their bodies have various patterns, colours and spotting which are often key to identification. Dolphins are generally social, capable of great speed, breathtaking acrobatics and bow-riding. They prey on a great variety of fish, squid and other marine life.

Long-snouted Spinner Dolphin

The mammal plates

The species illustrated Most of the species of mammal recorded in Galápagos are illustrated in the following plates. The only species to have been omitted are Longman's Beaked Whale and Ginkgo-toothed Beaked Whale, both of which may be present close to Galápagos, but have yet to be reliably sighted and photographed in the region.

The species order For ease of reference, the plates are ordered so that all the potential confusion species are together. The species are numbered sequentially and the text follows the order in which the species appear on the plate, from top to bottom. The species are numbered sequentially and the following annotations are used on the plates:

1 Adult (species 1)   1j Juvenile
1m Male   1f Female

Distribution maps A distribution map accompanies the text for the sea lions, rodents and bats. As with the maps used in the previous sections, three 'groups' of islands have been moved to save space (see page 33 for further details). The distribution of the species is shown in orange on the maps in this section, as in the 'dummy' map opposite.

English name The English names used in this book for the mammals are those most commonly used in recent literature.

Spanish name The Spanish names shown are those which are most regularly used in Galápagos.

Endemic species The names of species which are endemic to Galápagos are preceded by an **E**.

Status The first part of the text for each species provides information on its status.

This includes details of whether it is an indigenous resident, introduced, or migrant or vagrant, and a summary of their breeding season(s) and habitat preferences. The names of endemic subspecies are given in this section where appropriate.

Measurements The maximum recorded length of each species is given; in the case of cetaceans, the range of lengths of adults is shown.

Identification This section provides a summary of the key identification features, differences between males and females being described where necessary. In the case of cetaceans, details of the shape of the blow, the angle of breaching, whether the tail fluke is raised preceding a deep dive and the normal group size are given where this information aids identification.

Behaviour Particular behavioural characteristics which help in the identification of a species are highlighted where appropriate.

☐ Breeding range (regular)
· Colony
■ Regularly seen at sea
▨ Occasionally seen at sea
▨ Rarely seen at sea

PLATE 45

e **1** **Galápagos Sea Lion**   *Zalophus californianus*   Lobo Marino de Galápagos

Length: up to *c.* 230 cm

Weight: males up to 250 kg; females up to 120 kg

Common; endemic subspecies *wollebaeki* of the California Sea Lion, considered by some authorities to be a full species. Found in the shore zone and occasionally seen at sea away from land. Population estimated to number *c.* 50,000.

IDENTIFICATION: Large and conspicuous and rather thinly-furred. ADULT MALE: Considerably larger than female, with a steeply sloping forehead and raised crown, and a very thick neck when fully mature. Fur dark brown, often appearing black when wet. ADULT FEMALE: Considerably smaller than adult male and much more graceful, with a dog-like muzzle. Fur creamy brown, appearing dark brown when wet.

VOICE: A variety of rather high-pitched barking and yelping sounds.

BEHAVIOUR: Forms often large colonies on sandy beaches. Males are highly territorial, particularly during the mating season which runs from May to December, coinciding with the Garúa season, vigorously defending their territories against intruders. Males take up to ten years to become fully mature but are sexually active at about six or seven; females are fully mature at between six and eight years but can be sexually active at three years old. Pups are born during the Garúa season, although colonies on different islands give birth at different times, often up to three months apart. Immature males form discrete groups known as 'bachelor colonies'. Often very inquisitive and playful in the water and individuals regularly engage in body-surfing, often in a large wave. Feeds during the day.

E **2** **Galápagos Fur Seal**   *Arctocephalus galapagoensis*   Lobo de los Pelos

Length: up to *c.* 160 cm

Weight: males up to 75 kg; females up to 35 kg

Common. Found in the shore zone, mainly along rocky shores. Rarely seen at sea as feeds nocturnally. Population estimated to number *c.* 40,000.

IDENTIFICATION: Similar to Galápagos Sea Lion. Distinguished by its considerably smaller size, much thicker fur, proportionally shorter and broader head, more pointed nose, large and slightly bulging eyes with a glazed expression, prominent ears which tend to stick out from the head, and proportionally larger flippers. ADULT MALE: Considerably larger than female, with a thicker neck. Fur blackish to dark brown. ADULT FEMALE: Much smaller than adult male. Fur brown, sometimes with a slightly paler area on the nose and around the eyes.

VOICE: Less vocal than Galápagos Sea Lion, but the voice, although similar, is rather more guttural.

BEHAVIOUR: Forms small colonies on rocky shores, often lying in shady crevices during the heat of the day. Males are highly territorial, particularly during the mating season which runs from August to November, vigorously defending their territories against intruders. Males take five or six years to become fully mature; females are fully sexually mature at three years old. Most pups are born in October. Usually much shyer than the Galápagos Sea Lion. Feeds at night.

PLATE 46

E ❶ Santiago Rice Rat *Nesoryzomys swarthi*   Rata Endemica de Santiago

Length: up to 35 cm

Only rediscovered on Santiago in 1997, having not been recorded since 1906. Locally common in the arid zone to the north of the island. Although nothing is yet known about its biology or ecology this is the only species of rice rat which is known to have been able to compete successfully with the introduced Black Rat.

IDENTIFICATION: Similar in size and structure to the Large Fernandina Rice Rat. The fur is dark brown, although the underparts are pale and the feet are white. The tail is about the same length as the head and body.

BEHAVIOUR: Active at night.

E ❷ Small Fernandina Rice Rat *Nesoryzomys fernandinae*   Raton Endemico de Fernandina

Length: up to 22 cm

Only recently described, having been recorded only from owl pellets until 1995 when the first live animals were trapped. Confined to Fernandina. Probably locally common, particularly at higher elevations, although nothing is yet known about its biology or ecology.

IDENTIFICATION: Considerably smaller than the Large Fernandina Rice Rat, from which it is distinguished by its darker, brownish fur and dark, rather than white, feet. The tail is slightly shorter than the length of the head and body.

BEHAVIOUR: Active at night.

E ❸ Large Fernandina Rice Rat *Nesoryzomys narboroughii*   Rata Endemica de Fernandina

Length: up to 35 cm

Locally common throughout the island, particularly in the arid zone. Confined to Fernandina. Little is known about the biology or ecology of this species, although it is believed to breed principally during the warm/wet season.

IDENTIFICATION: Considerably larger than the Small Fernandina Rice Rat, from which it is distinguished by its paler, greyish-black fur with pale underparts, and white feet. The tail is about the same length as the head and body.

BEHAVIOUR: Active at night and therefore rarely seen by visitors; feeds on the ground.

E ❹ Santa Fé Rice Rat *Oryzomys bauri*   Rata Endemica de Santa Fé

Length: up to 20 cm

Locally common, particularly in the arid zone. Confined to Santa Fé, where it is free from the depredations of Black Rat. Breeding takes place during the warm/wet season.

IDENTIFICATION: The Santa Fé Rice Rat is a small, brown rat with a pointed nose; long legs; long, pale but black-soled hindfeet; and pale underparts. They have large, rather bulging eyes and the ears are large and sparsely-haired. The tail is about the same length as the head and body, and is slender and naked.

BEHAVIOUR: Unafraid of humans but active principally at night and therefore rarely seen by visitors. When active, they spend their time on the ground.

PLATE 47

❶ Hoary Bat *Lasiurus cinereus* Murciélago Escarchado

Size: Large (length of forearm: *c.* 55 mm)

Locally common.

IDENTIFICATION: Short, blunt head and ears, no nose-leaf, and thickly-furred tail membrane. Considerably larger than Galápagos Bat. A large bat that tends to fly high off the ground, usually above *c.* 8 m, with a strong, fast flight and slow wingbeats. Fur light brown, with white 'frosting' and a white throat.

BEHAVIOUR: Like the Galápagos Bat, roosts in trees in sheltered places, especially in mangroves and along forest edges; usually occurring singly. Occasionally forages around street lights in towns.

ⓔ ❷ Galápagos Red Bat *Lasiurus borealis* Murciélago Vespertino Galápagueño

Size: Small (length of forearm: *c.* 40 mm)

Locally common resident; endemic subspecies brachyotis, which is considered by some authorities to be a full species. Found in both the highlands and lowlands.

IDENTIFICATION: Short, blunt head and ears, no nose-leaf, and thickly-furred tail membrane. Considerably smaller than Hoary Bat. Tends to fly relatively close to the ground, with rather fast wing-beats. Fur bright rusty-orange on lower back; forequarters yellow, frosted with red; underparts yellowish.

BEHAVIOUR: A tree-roosting bat, usually occurring singly among foliage in sheltered places, especially along forest edges. Occasionally forages around street lights in towns.

❸ House Mouse *Mus musculus* Raton

Length: up to 9·5 cm

Introduced to many of the islands in Galápagos and included here to enable a comparison to be made with the rice rats. Nocturnal, mainly terrestrial.

IDENTIFICATION: Distinguished by its very small size and dark brownish-grey fur with slightly paler underparts. The tail is about the same length as the body.

❹ Black (or Ship) Rat *Rattus rattus* Rata Negra

Length: *c.* 35 cm

Introduced to many of the islands in Galápagos, where it has had a devastating effect on many animal communities. Apart from on Santiago, no native rodents survive today on islands where Black Rats are present. Although an introduced species, the Black Rat is included in this book to enable a comparison to be made with the rice rats. Nocturnal, mainly terrestrial, but very capable climbers.

INTRODUCED SPECIES

▫ Black Rat and House Mouse

▪ Brown Rat

IDENTIFICATION: Upperparts black or dark grey, or tawny-brown; underparts grey. The tail is longer than the length of the head and body and the whiskers are long, reaching as far as the shoulders. The ears are of medium length.

❺ Brown (or Norway) Rat *Rattus norvegicus* Rata Doméstica

Length: *c.* 4 cm

Introduced to some of the islands where it is found mainly in areas of human habitation. Although an introduced species, the Brown Rat is included in this book to enable a comparison to be made with the rice rats. Nocturnal, mainly terrestrial.

IDENTIFICATION: Similar to tawny-brown form of Black Rat but generally larger, with tail shorter than the length of the head and body, shorter whiskers that reach only as far as the ears, and proportionally shorter ears.

PLATE 48

① Minke Whale   *Balaenoptera acutorostrata*   Rorcual Aliblanco

Adult Length: 7–10 m

Blow: Small, vertical and bushy but usually not visible

Breaching: Variable angles

Deep dive: Tail flukes not raised

Group size: 1–2

Rare offshore.

IDENTIFICATION: The smallest of its family, similar in size and shape to the beaked whales but its pointed snout, with a single ridge on the upper surface, distinguishes it from toothed cetaceans. Differs from other rorquals in its small size, lack of a tall blow, and large dorsal fin in relation to body length. Like the Sei Whale, the dorsal fin usually appears at the same time as the blowholes on surfacing. Many individuals show a white flipper band which is diagnostic.

② Sei Whale   *Balaenoptera borealis*   Rorcual Boreal

Adult Length: 12–16 m

Blow: Tall, thin and vertical – less robust than Fin Whale

Breaching: Seldom, generally rising at a low angle

Deep dive: Does not raise tail flukes

Group size: 1–2, sometimes more when feeding

Rare offshore.

IDENTIFICATION: Very similar to Bryde's Whale both in size and appearance, but the single ridge on top of the head distinguishes it at close range. Differs from Minke Whale in size and presence of tall, visible blow, and from Fin and Blue Whales by surfacing sequence and taller, more sickle-shaped fin. On surfacing, dorsal fin breaks the surface at the same time as the blowholes.

③ Bryde's Whale   *Balaenoptera edeni*   Rorcual Tropical

Adult Length: 11–15 m

Blow: Tall, thin and vertical

Breaching: Usually leaves water at a steep angle

Deep dive: Unlike Sei Whale, often arches tail stock before dive; does not raise tail flukes

Group size: 1–2, sometimes more when feeding

Frequent inshore and offshore.

IDENTIFICATION: Easily confused with the Sei Whale due to its similar size, shape, and sickle-shaped dorsal fin. However, it possesses three lateral raised ridges on top of its head ③r, a feature which distinguishes it from all other rorquals which only have a single ridge. The surfacing sequence is also unique, with the blowholes disappearing from view just before the fin appears. This feature alone should not be used for identification.

④ Fin Whale   *Balaenoptera physalus*   Rorcual Común

Adult Length: 18–26 m

Blow: Tall column, thicker and higher than Sei and Bryde's Whales but smaller than Blue Whale

Breaching: Variable angles, huge splash

Deep dive: Tail flukes not raised

Group size: 1–2, sometimes more when feeding

Rare offshore.

IDENTIFICATION: Second only to the Blue Whale in size, Fin Whales are similar to the other large rorquals. At close quarters, the asymmetrical pigmentation of the lower jaw is diagnostic. The left lower lip ④l is dark, whilst the right ④r is white. Surfacing sequence is distinctive: appearance of blowholes precedes a rolling back, followed by the small but distinct sloping dorsal fin.

PLATE 49

❶ Blue Whale *Balaenoptera musculus* Ballena Azul

Adult Length: 24–30 m

Blow: Largest of all: an enormous vertical column up to 10 m tall

Breaching: Only young known to breach, usually at 45° angle

Deep dive: Sometimes raises tail flukes

Group size: 1–2, sometimes more when feeding

Rare offshore.

IDENTIFICATION: The Blue Whale is the largest animal on the planet, but its size is not the easiest feature with which to distinguish it. Instead, concentrate on surfacing sequence, fin size, and coloration. Confusion is most likely with the Fin Whale but on surfacing a Blue Whale exhales an even larger blow. The head then disappears to reveal a long rolling back before, finally, a tiny, stubby dorsal fin appears just before the animal sinks below the surface. Body colour is bluish-grey but, unlike Fin Whale, it is usually covered with pale mottling.

❷ Humpback Whale *Megaptera novaeangliae* Jorobada

Adult Length: 11–15 m

Blow: Variable; tall, vertical and bushy

Breaching: Yes, usually landing on back

Deep dive: Body generally arches high before broad tail flukes are raised to reveal variable pale underside to tail

Group size: 1–3, sometimes more when feeding

Occasional inshore and offshore.

IDENTIFICATION: Although similar to the other rorquals in size, the Humpback Whale is one of the most distinctive species. Its scientific name means 'Big-winged New Englander', a description referring to its huge flippers which are over 3 m long. Surfacing sequence is slow, the head is covered in raised knobs and the body is robust and bulky, with a low, sloping and broad-based dorsal fin. The back behind the fin, like the Sperm Whale, shows a series of knuckles along its ridge.

❸ Sperm Whale *Physeter macrocephalus* (formerly *P. catodon*) Cachalote

Adult Length: 11–18 m

Blow: Single blowhole on left side of head; blow angled forward and to the left

Breaching: Frequent, most of body leaves water

Deep dive: Often arches body; usually raises dark, broad, triangular tail flukes vertically

Group size: Group size: 1–20, sometimes more

Frequent offshore.

The abundance of Sperm Whales in this region made it the focus of the whaling industry in the nineteenth century, and of extensive research in recent years. The seas around Galápagos form important feeding and breeding grounds for this species. Since the late 1980s numbers have declined from a few hundred to generally 10–20 in the 1990s. The reason for this change is unknown.

IDENTIFICATION: The Sperm Whale is the largest toothed whale, overlapping with several rorquals in size. However, its squarish head, blow, and wrinkled skin make it very distinctive. At the surface it generally shows a low-lying, straight back. There is a small hump instead of a fin, behind which are a series of knuckles running as far as the tail.

PLATE 50

❶ Dwarf Sperm Whale — *Kogia simus* — Cachalote Enaño

Adult Length: 2·1–2·8 m
Blow: Blowhole displaced slightly to the left; blow low and faint
Breaching: Leaps vertically
Deep dive: Tail flukes not raised
Group size: 1–10

Occasional offshore and inshore.

IDENTIFICATION: Very similar to Pygmy Sperm Whale (see identification notes for that species) but marginally smaller and best identified by its slightly larger dorsal fin positioned centrally on the back. Identification remains very difficult without exceptionally good views and consequently observations at sea are often recorded as Pygmy/Dwarf Sperm Whale.

❷ Pygmy Sperm Whale — *Kogia breviceps* — Cachalote Pigmeo

Adult Length: 2·7–3·7 m
Blow: Blowhole displaced slightly to the left; blow low and faint
Breaching: Leaps vertically
Deep dive: Tail flukes not raised
Group size: 1–6

Rare offshore.

IDENTIFICATION: The small size of the Pygmy Sperm Whale means that it is most likely to be mistaken for a dolphin, although its blunt, squarish head, robust body, small dorsal fin and behaviour are distinctive. However, it is extremely similar to the Dwarf Sperm Whale. Both species are typically seen travelling slowly or hanging motionless at the surface and on diving, simply sink below the surface rather than rolling forward. Both are also usually shy of boats and, when disturbed, excrete a reddish-brown ink in defence. The Pygmy Sperm Whale is slightly larger but the size and position of the dorsal fin is the key feature, being smaller and positioned further than halfway along the back.

❸ Blainville's Beaked Whale — *Mesoplodon densirostris* — Zifio de Blainville

Adult Length: 4–6 m
Coloration: Blue-grey to orange-brown
Blow: Small blow projects forward, sometimes visible
Breaching: Unknown
Group size: 1–6

Occasional offshore.

IDENTIFICATION: Very similar in shape and size to other beaked whales of the genus *Mesoplodon*. Identification requires close views of the beak which appears first as the animal surfaces. The forehead is low and flat leading to a shortish beak, behind which both sides of the lower jaw are distinctly arched towards the base. Unlike Gingko-toothed Beaked Whale the arch is rounded. Mature males display a large single tooth, irrupting from the centre of each arch.

Ginkgo-toothed Beaked Whale — *Mesoplodon ginkgodens* — Zifio Japoné

Adult Length: 5 m
Coloration: Uniformly dark
Blow: Unknown
Breaching: Unknown
Group size: Unknown

Status unknown: 1 stranding, on Genovesa, in June 1970.

IDENTIFICATION: Similar in body shape to Blainville's Beaked Whale, so close views of the head are required for identification. The forehead slopes smoothly into the upper jaw, forming a prominent beak. Both sides of the lower jaw rise steeply halfway along the beak before levelling out at eye height. This gives the beak an angled, arched appearance which, unlike Blainville's, does not protrude above the upper jaw. In older males, a single tooth (the base of which is shaped like the leaf of a Ginkgo Tree) irrupts from the tip of each arch.

❹ Cuvier's Beaked Whale — *Ziphius cavirostris* — Zifio Común

Adult Length: 5–7 m
Coloration: Grey-brown to brick-red
Blow: Bushy, slightly angled forward, sometimes visible
Breaching: Leaps almost vertically
Group size: 1–8

Occasional offshore.

IDENTIFICATION: Larger and more robust than the beaked whales of the genus *Mesoplodon*. The body is somewhat sausage-shaped as it rolls slowly at the surface, revealing a small, triangular or falcate dorsal fin situated two-thirds of the way along the back. The head shape is distinctive, the forehead sloping gently down to a short beak, described by some as being like that of a goose. In mature males, two small teeth protrude from the tip of the lower jaw. The head and upper back of adults often becomes pale cream in colour.

PLATE 51

❶ Killer Whale (or Orca)   *Orcinus orca*   Orca

Adult Length: 5–9 m
Blow: Tall and bushy
Breaching: Leaps vertically
Group size: Family groups of 2–30

Frequent inshore and offshore.

IDENTIFICATION: The largest of the dolphins and perhaps the most distinctive cetacean of all. The striking black body, white eye-patch and prominent dorsal fin are unmistakable. Dorsal fin size and shape varies with age and sex. Adult males possess triangular fins which can reach up to 2m in height. Females and immatures have smaller, sickle-shaped fins. Known to hunt other marine mammals including Sperm Whales and Bryde's Whales in Galápagos.

❷ False Killer Whale   *Pseudorca crassidens*   Falsa Orca

Adult Length: 4–6 m
Blow: Inconspicuous and bushy
Breaching: Frequent, various angles
Group size: 2–200

Occasional inshore and offshore.

IDENTIFICATION: Similar in shape to Melon-headed Whale and Pygmy Killer Whale but much larger and more powerful. Confusion is perhaps most likely with female Orca or Short-finned Pilot Whale. With good views the all-dark body distinguishes it from the former, and its slender, rounded head and body, with a dolphin-like dorsal fin, separates it from the latter. The position of the dorsal fin also differs from that of the Pilot Whale, being set further back at the mid-point of the back. At the surface False Killer Whales are often highly active swimmers, lifting their whole heads and bodies out of the water whilst travelling. Known to attack other cetaceans, including Sperm Whales, in Galápagos.

❸ Short-finned Pilot Whale   *Globicephala macrorhyncus*   Calderon Tropical

Adult Length: 3·5–6·5 m
Blow: Distinctly bushy
Breaching: Occasional, various angles
Group size: Family groups of 2–50

Occasional inshore and offshore.

IDENTIFICATION: The Short-finned Pilot Whale is one of the easiest species to identify due to its characteristic shape and behaviour. On surfacing, the bulbous, rounded head precedes a robust body with a dorsal fin set well forward. Behind the dorsal fin is a pale 'saddle patch' followed by a long back and tail stock. In both sexes the dorsal fin is very broad at the base, but this is especially so in adult males which have a large, flag-shaped fin. Because they tend to feed at night, most of the day is spent either travelling at a leisurely pace or logging.

❹ Melon-headed Whale   *Peponocephala electra*   Calderon Pequeño

Adult Length: 2–2·7 m
Blow: Generally not visible
Breaching: Occasional
Group size: Generally 50+

Rare offshore.

IDENTIFICATION: This small, slender species is akin in size and shape to most dolphins. However its all-black coloration and lack of a prominent beak distinguish it. Confusion is most likely with the Pygmy Killer Whale which is extremely similar. Close views in good light are required but there are several subtle differences. Perhaps most diagnostic is head shape which is slightly pointed or 'melon-shaped'. Other differences include slimmer and more sharply pointed flippers, lack of a dark cape, and a short but distinct beak, often present on females and juveniles.

❺ Pygmy Killer Whale   *Feresa attenuata*   Orca Pigmea

Adult Length: 2–2·7 m
Blow: Generally not visible
Breaching: Occasional
Group size: Generally 1–50

Rare offshore.

IDENTIFICATION: Only likely to be confused with the Melon-headed Whale, as its all-dark, grey-black coloration and lack of a beak distinguishes it from the dolphins. The similarity with Melon-headed Whale means that close views are required for positive identification. Head shape is an important feature to note, being distinctly rounded in Pygmy Killer Whales. Another significant difference is the black cape, which reaches its maximum width below the dorsal fin, and is distinctive in some animals. Some individuals may also have white chins. The flippers are rounded at the tips.

PLATE 52

❶ Common Dolphin *Delphinus delphis* Delfín Común

Adult Length: 1·7–2·4 m
Behaviour: Highly active, fast swimmer capable of impressive acrobatics
Group size: 1–2,000

Frequent offshore, occasional inshore.

IDENTIFICATION: This small and acrobatic dolphin is very similar in shape to the Striped Dolphin and Pantropical Spotted Dolphin, so identification in poor light can be difficult. In good light this species is easily identified by its coloration and patterning. The dorsal fin and cape are black, with the cape dropping to form a 'V'-shape on the flanks below the dorsal fin. The flank is coloured in a criss-crossed pattern with yellow-buff from the eye to the dorsal fin, and with grey between the dorsal fin and the tail. The base of the dorsal fin is often pale and a black line runs between the beak and the flipper.

❷ Striped Dolphin *Stenella coeruleoalba* Delfín Listado

Adult Length: 1·8–2·5 m
Behaviour: Perhaps even more acrobatic than the Common Dolphin, sometimes breaching as high as 7m. Often cautious around boats, swimming in a tightly-packed pod
Group size: Generally 10–500

Occasional offshore.

IDENTIFICATION: Due to similarities in size, shape and behaviour with Common and Pantropical Spotted Dolphins, pattern and colour are key to the identification of this small, slender cetacean. A thin dark body-stripe runs along a pale flank from behind the eye to the tail stock, and another stripe runs from the eye to the flipper giving the Striped Dolphin its name. Surprisingly, this is not the most reliable identification feature because both stripes remain below the surface when individuals are not porpoising. Fortunately, the dark grey cape on the upper back is distinctive, being dissected by a pale strip angled backwards towards the dorsal fin.

❸ Long-snouted Spinner Dolphin *Stenella longirostris* Estenela Giradora

Adult Length: 1·5–2·2 m
Behaviour: One of the most acrobatic of all dolphins, capable of twisting its body longitudinally to spin up to 7 times in a single leap
Group size: Generally 5–200

Occasional offshore.

IDENTIFICATION: This small, streamlined dolphin with a long beak and lack of patterning is only likely to be confused with the Pantropical Spotted Dolphin. There are three distinct races in the eastern tropical Pacific which are likely to occur in Galápagos and these vary in colour and beak length. Colour varies from uniform dark grey to bicoloured or tricoloured shades of grey, fading paler towards the belly. In mature males the dorsal fin is often an erect triangular shape or angled slightly forward, giving the impression that the fin is on backwards! Older males also develop a distinct anterior bulge under the tail stock. This is unique and clearly visible in leaping dolphins. Spinner Dolphins are often characterised by their crazy spinning behaviour.

❹ Pantropical Spotted Dolphin *Stenella attenuata* Delfín Moteado

Adult Length: 1·7–2·4 m
Behaviour: Highly energetic and acrobatic
Group size: Generally 50–1,000

Occasional offshore.

IDENTIFICATION: Very similar to Common and Striped Dolphins in shape but lacks flank markings. Instead, the dark dorsal fin and cape give way to lighter grey flanks and a pale grey belly (the belly is white in Common and Striped Dolphins). A dark band runs between the beak and the dark flipper. Calves are unspotted at birth but become more spotted with age until, in adulthood, the body is completely covered. Often occurs in mixed pods with Long-snouted Spinner Dolphins but are easily told apart by the spotting and curved dorsal fin.

PLATE 53

❶ Risso's Dolphin *Grampus griseus* Delfín Gris

Adult Length: 2·6–3·8 m

Behaviour: Can be energetic but more frequently engages in slow travel or logging. Displays many behaviours including spy-hopping, lobtailing and breaching

Group size: 1–500

Occasional offshore.

IDENTIFICATION: The distinctive colour and shape of the Risso's Dolphin means that it is unlikely to be mistaken given good views. In shape it is perhaps more reminiscent of a blackfish than a dolphin due to its large size, bulbous head, short indistinct beak and prominent falcate dorsal fin. However, the extensive scarring and whitish skin are diagnostic (although a similar pattern is exhibited by mature Cuvier's Beaked Whales). Born pale grey, the body darkens until maturity, then lightens to a creamy white. By this time the body tends to be covered in scratch marks from infighting and scars inflicted by their squid prey. Adults become continually paler with age but the dorsal fin and adjacent back often remain dark.

❷ Bottle-nosed Dolphin *Tursiops truncatus* Delfín Mular

Adult Length: 1·9–3·90 m

Behaviour: Highly active, capable of great speed and amazing acrobatics

Group size: 1–25

Frequent inshore and offshore.

IDENTIFICATION: Due to its popularity in aquaria and with the media, this is perhaps the most familiar of all the dolphins. It is also one of the most distinctive. Bottle-nosed Dolphins are large, robust animals which move powerfully through the water. Their size and plain grey coloration, paler below but with no distinct flank markings, set them apart from all but the Rough-toothed Dolphin. However, the distinct bulging forehead and short, stubby beak distinguish it from Rough-toothed.

❸ Fraser's Dolphin *Lagenodelphis hosei* Delfín de Fraser

Adult Length: 2–2·6 m

Behaviour: Powerful swimming style, often leaving the water in a burst of spray

Group size: 100–500

Rare offshore.

IDENTIFICATION: Although amongst the least known of all dolphins, Fraser's Dolphin has a distinctive shape. It appears robust towards the head, slender behind the small, curved dorsal fin, and has a short beak. These characteristics are intermediate between the genera *Lagenorhyncus* and *Delphinus*, hence the species' scientific name. Flank patterning is also very distinctive. Some individuals, especially males, have a thick, dark lateral body-stripe which runs from the eye backwards and is bordered by a pale stripe above and a pale belly below. Another dark line runs from the beak to the flippers. The strength of the stripe varies greatly from individual to individual, but at least some dolphins in a pod generally show strong markings.

❹ Rough-toothed Dolphin *Steno bredanensis* Steno

Adult Length: 2·1–2·6 m

Behaviour: Sometimes shows a characteristic swimming pattern described as 'skimming across the surface'

Group size: 1–50

Rare: 1 stranding, at Tortuga Bay, Santa Cruz Island in 1964.

IDENTIFICATION: Wholly dark grey body makes confusion with Spotted, Spinner and Bottle-nosed Dolphins and the smaller blackfish possible. The narrow elongated beak is the most distinctive feature, tapering gradually from the forehead to give a cone-shaped impression. All other dolphins have a clear demarcation between the forehead and beak. The beak also often shows whitish or pinkish patches, particularly around the lips, but this may extend to a white throat. Below the tall prominent dorsal fin is a narrow dark cape, a feature which is lacking in the uniformly coloured Bottle-nosed Dolphin.

CHECKLIST OF THE REGULARLY OCCURRING SPECIES

WITH SUMMARY OF HABITAT PREFERENCES AND DISTRIBUTION

KEY TO THE TABLE

The symbols used for species' status:

E species endemic to the Galápagos
e subspecies endemic to the Galápagos
r resident species
m regular migrant
i introduced species
? status uncertain

The symbols used in the habitat preference columns:

■ favoured habitat
▪ sometimes recorded

The symbols used in the islands columns:

● breeds
· occurs but does not breed or is uncommon
✳ breeds only on satellite islands
? status uncertain
▮ occurs in the waters around the island
▬ migrant, may be found in coastal waters
▬ migrant, may be found in suitable habitat on any island

ssp. denotes endemic subspecies where more than one occurs in the Galápagos

		Habitat preference						Islands										
		Open sea	Rocky islets	Shore zone	Arid zone	Transition zone	Humid zone	Española (Hood)	Floreana (Charles)	San Cristóbal (Chatham)	Santa Fé (Barrington)	Santa Cruz (Indefatigable)	Baltra & Seymour	Pinzón (Duncan)	Isabela (Albemarle)	Fernandina (Narborough)	Santiago (James)	Genovesa (Tower)
	BIRDS																	
✓	**Seabirds**																	
E	Albatross, Waved	■			■			●										
e	Booby, Blue-footed	■	■	■	■			●	●	●	●	✳	●	●	●	●	●	●
r	Booby, Nazca	■	■	■	■			●	✳	✳								●
r	Booby, Red-footed	■	■	■	■					✳								●
E	Cormorant, Flightless	▪													●	●		
r	Frigatebird, Great	■	■	■	■			●	●	✳		●	●	●	●		●	●
e	Frigatebird, Magnificent	■	■	■	■			●	●	●	●	●	●	●	●	●	●	●
m	Gull, Franklin's	■	▪	■														
m	Gull, Laughing	■	▪	■														
E	Gull, Lava	■	■	■				·	·	●	·	●	●	·	●	●	●	·
E	Gull, Swallow-tailed	■	■	■	▪			●	●	●	●	●	●	●	●	●	●	●
m	Jaeger, Pomarine	■																
e	Noddy, Common	■	■	■	▪			●	●	●	●	●	●	●	●	●	●	●
e	Pelican, Brown	■	■	■	▪			●	●	●	●	●	●	●	●		●	●
E	Penguin, Galápagos	■	■	■											●	●		
e	Petrel, Dark-rumped (or Galápagos)	■					■	●	●	●		●			●		●	
E	Shearwater, Galápagos	■	■	■	▪			●	●	●	●	●	●	●	●	●	●	●
m	Shearwater, Sooty	■																
e	Storm-petrel, Elliot's (or White-vented)	■																
r	Storm-petrel, Madeiran	■	■	▪	■			●	✳	✳		✳			✳		✳	✳
m	Storm-petrel, Markham's	■																
e	Storm-petrel, Wedge-rumped	■																
m	Tern, Common	■	▪															
m	Tern, Royal	■	▪															
r	Tern, Sooty	■	■									Darwin only						
r	Tropicbird, Red-billed	■	■	■	▪			●	●	●	●	●	●	●	●	●	●	●

		Habitat preference						Islands										
		Open sea	Rocky islets	Shore zone	Arid zone	Transition zone	Humid zone	Española (Hood)	Floreana (Charles)	San Cristóbal (Chatham)	Santa Fé (Barrington)	Santa Cruz (Indefatigable)	Baltra & Seymour	Pinzón (Duncan)	Isabela (Albemarle)	Fernandina (Narborough)	Santiago (James)	Genovesa (Tower)
✓	**WATERBIRDS**																	
r	Crake, Paint-billed				▪	■	▪		●	●		●			●			
r	Egret, Cattle			■	▪	■	▪		●	●		●	•		●		•	•
r	Egret, Great			■	▪	■	▪		•	●	•	●	•	•	●		•	
m	Egret, Snowy			■														
r	Flamingo, Greater			■					●			●			●		●	
r	Gallinule, Common (or Moorhen)			■					●	●		●			●		•	
e	Heron, Great Blue			■					●	●	•	●	•	•	•			
E	Heron, Lava (or Galápagos)			■				●	●	●	●	●	●	●	●	●	●	●
r	Heron, Striated			■	▪					●		●			●		●	
e	Night-heron, Yellow-crowned		▪	■				●	●	●	●	●	●	●	●	●	●	●
e	Pintail, White-cheeked (or Galápagos)			■		■		•	●	●	•	●	•	•	●	●	●	•
E	Rail, Galápagos					▪	■		•	?		●			●		●	
m	Teal, Blue-winged			▪	■	■												
	SHOREBIRDS																	
m	Dowitcher, Short-billed			■														
e	Oystercatcher, American		▪	■				•	●	●	•	●	•	•	●	●	●	•
m	Phalarope, Red (or Grey)	■		▪														
m	Phalarope, Red-necked	■		▪														
m	Phalarope, Wilson's			■														
m	Plover, Black-bellied (or Grey)			■														
m	Plover, Semipalmated			■														
m	Sanderling			■														
m	Sandpiper, Least			■														
m	Sandpiper, Solitary			■		■	▪											
m	Sandpiper, Spotted			■														
r	Stilt, Black-necked			■		■	▪		●	●	•	●	•	•	●		●	
m	Surfbird			■														
m	Tattler, Wandering			■														
m	Turnstone, Ruddy			■														
m	Whimbrel			■		■	▪											
m	Willet			■														
m	Yellowlegs, Lesser			■														
	RAPTORS																	
E	Hawk, Galápagos				■	■	■	●			●	•		●	●	●	●	
m	Osprey		▪		■	▪												
m	Peregrine		▪		■	▪												
	NIGHTBIRDS																	
e	Owl, Barn				■	■	▪			●		●	•		●		●	●
e	Owl, Short-eared			▪	■	■	■	●	●	●	●	●	●	●	●	●	●	●
	LARGER LANDBIRDS																	
r?	Ani, Groove-billed				▪	■	▪					?						
r	Ani, Smooth-billed				▪	■	▪		●			●						
r	Cuckoo, Dark-billed			▪	▪	■	■		●	●		●	•	•	•		●	
E	Dove, Galápagos		▪	▪	■	▪		●	•	?	●	•		•	•	•	●	●
m	Kingfisher, Belted			■														
	AERIAL FEEDERS																	
E	Martin, Galápagos			■	■	■	■		•	●		●		•	●	●	●	●
m	Swallow, Barn				■	■	■											

		Habitat preference						Islands										
		Open sea	Rocky islets	Shore zone	Arid zone	Transition zone	Humid zone	Española (Hood)	Floreana (Charles)	San Cristóbal (Chatham)	Santa Fé (Barrington)	Santa Cruz (Indefatigable)	Baltra & Seymour	Pinzón (Duncan)	Isabela (Albemarle)	Fernandina (Narborough)	Santiago (James)	Genovesa (Tower)

✓ SMALLER LANDBIRDS

Status	Name	Notes
E	Finch, Cactus ssp. *abingdoni*	Pinta only
	ssp. *intermedia*	
	ssp. *rothschildi*	Marchena only
	ssp. *scandens*	
E	Finch, Large Cactus ssp. *conirostris*	
	ssp. *darwinii*	Darwin and Wolf only
	ssp. *propinqua*	
E	Finch, Large Ground	
E	Finch, Large Tree ssp. *affinis*	
	ssp. *habeli*	Pinta and Marchena only
	ssp. *psittacula*	
E	Finch, Mangrove	
E	Finch, Medium Ground	
E	Finch, Medium Tree	
E	Finch, Sharp-beaked Ground	
	ssp. *debilirostris*	
	ssp. *difficilis*	also Pinta
	ssp. *septentrionalis*	Darwin and Wolf only
E	Finch, Small Ground	
E	Finch, Small Tree ssp. *parvulus*	
	ssp. *salvini*	
E	Finch, Vegetarian	
E	Finch, Warbler ssp. *becki*	Darwin and Wolf only
	ssp. *bifasciata*	
	ssp. *cinerascens*	
	ssp. *fusca*	Pinta and Marchena only
	ssp. *luteola*	
	ssp. *mentalis*	
	ssp. *olivacea*	
	ssp. *ridgwayii*	
E	Finch, Woodpecker ssp. *pallidus*	
	ssp. *productus*	
	ssp. *striatipectus*	
E	Flycatcher, Large-billed (or Galápagos)	
e	Flycatcher, Vermilion ssp. *dubius*	San Cristóbal only - possibly **EXTINCT**
	ssp. *nanus*	
E	Mockingbird, Charles (or Floreana)	
E	Mockingbird, Chatham	
E	Mockingbird, Galápagos ssp. *bauri*	
	ssp. *barringtoni*	
	ssp. *hulli*	Darwin only
	ssp. *parvulus*	
	ssp. *personatus*	also Pinta, Marchena and Rábida
	ssp. *wenmani*	Wolf only
E	Mockingbird, Hood	
e	Warbler, Yellow	

REPTILES

		Open sea	Rocky islets	Shore zone	Arid zone	Transition zone	Humid zone	Española (Hood)	Floreana (Charles)	San Cristóbal (Chatham)	Santa Fé (Barrington)	Santa Cruz (Indefatigable)	Baltra & Seymour	Pinzón (Duncan)	Isabela (Albemarle)	Fernandina (Narborough)	Santiago (James)	Genovesa (Tower)
✓	**TORTOISE**																	
E	Tortoise, Galápagos ssp. *abingdoni*							Pinta only - **EXTINCT in the wild**										
	ssp. *becki*				▪	■	■								●			
	ssp. *chathamensis*				▪	■	■			●								
	ssp. *darwini*				▪	■	■										●	
	ssp. *elephantopus*					■	■								●			
	ssp. *ephippium*				▪	■	■							●				
	ssp. *guntheri*				▪	■	■								●			
	ssp. *hoodensis*					■			●									
	ssp. *microphyes*				▪	■	■								●			
	ssp. *porteri*				▪	■	■						●					
	ssp. *vandenburghi*				▪	■	■								●			
	TURTLES																	
r	Turtle, Black (or Pacific Green)	■		■				●	●	●	●	●	●		●	●	●	●
m	Turtle, Hawksbill	■																
m	Turtle, Loggerhead	■																
m	Turtle, Olive Ridley	■																
	GECKOS																	
E	Leaf-toed Gecko, Baur's			■	■	■		●	●									
E	Leaf-toed Gecko, Galápagos			■	■	■						?	●	?	●	●	●	●
E	Leaf-toed Gecko, Rábida				■	■		Rábida only - possibly **EXTINCT**										
E	Leaf-toed Gecko, San Cristóbal				■	■				●								
E	Leaf-toed Gecko, Santa Fé				■	■					●							
r	Leaf-toed Gecko, Tuberculated				■	■				●								
E	Leaf-toed Gecko, Wenman				■	■		Wolf only										
i	*Gonatodes caudiscutatus*			Buildings						●								
i	*Lepidodactylus lugubris*			Buildings						●								
i	*Phyllodactylus reissi*			Buildings						●								
	LIZARDS																	
E	Lava Lizard, Española			■	■	■		●										
E	Lava Lizard, Floreana			■	■	■			●									
E	Lava Lizard, Galápagos			■	■	■		& Rábida		●	●	●			●	●	●	●
E	Lava Lizard, Marchena			■	■			Marchena only										
E	Lava Lizard, Pinta			■	■			Pinta only										
E	Lava Lizard, Pinzón				■	■								●				
E	Lava Lizard, San Cristóbal				■	■				●								
	IGUANAS																	
E	Iguana, Land				■	■						●	●		●		●	
E	Iguana, Marine ssp. *albemarlensis*	▪	■	■	▪										●			
	ssp. *cristatus*	▪	■	■	▪												●	
	ssp. *hassi*	▪	■	■	▪				?		?	●	?	?				
	ssp. *mertensi*	▪	■	■	▪					●							●	
	ssp. *nanus*	▪	■	■	▪													●
	ssp. *sielmanni*	▪	■	■	▪			Pinta only										
	ssp. *venustissimus*	▪	■	■	▪			●										
E	Iguana, Santa Fé Land				■	■					●							

153

✓		HABITAT PREFERENCE						ISLANDS										
		Open sea	Rocky islets	Shore zone	Arid zone	Transition zone	Humid zone	Española (Hood)	Floreana (Charles)	San Cristóbal (Chatham)	Santa Fé (Barrington)	Santa Cruz (Indefatigable)	Baltra & Seymour	Pinzón (Duncan)	Isabela (Albemarle)	Fernandina (Narborough)	Santiago (James)	Genovesa (Tower)
	SNAKES																	
E	Snake, Floreana		■	■	■				●									
	—, Española		■	■	■			●										
	—, San Cristóbal		■	■	■					●								
E	Snake, Galápagos		■	■	■							● & Rábida	●	●			●	
	—, Fernandina		■	■	■											●		
	—, Isabela		■	■	■										●			
E	Snake, Slevin's		■	■	■									●	●	●		
	—, Steindachner's		■	■	■							● & Rábida	●				●	
m	Snake, Yellow-bellied Sea	■																
	MAMMALS																	
	SEA LIONS																	
E	Fur Seal, Galápagos	■	■	■	■			●	●	●	●	●	●	●	●	●	●	●
e	Sea Lion, Galápagos	■	■	■	■			●	●	●	●	●	●	●	●	●	●	●
	RICE RATS																	
E	Rice Rat, Large Fernandina			▪	■	■	■									●		
E	Rice Rat, Santa Fé			▪	■						●							
E	Rice Rat, Santiago			▪	■												●	
E	Rice Rat, Small Fernandina			▪	■	■										●		
	INTRODUCED RODENTS																	
i	Mouse, House			■	■	■	■		●	●		●	●		●		●	●
i	Rat, Black (or Ship)			■	■	■	■		●	●		●	●		●		●	●
i	Rat, Brown (or Norway)	Towns & habitations								●		●			?			
	BATS																	
r	Bat, Hoary			■	■	■	■		●	●		●			●		●	
e	Bat, Galápagos Red			■	■	■	■			●		●						
	WHALES																	
?	Whale, Blainville's Beaked	■																
r	Whale, Bryde's	■																
?	Whale, Cuvier's Beaked	■																
m	Whale, False Killer	■																
m	Whale, Humpback	■																
r	Whale, Killer (or Orca)	■																
r	Whale, Short-finned Pilot	■																
r	Whale, Sperm	■																
	DOLPHINS																	
r	Dolphin, Bottle-nosed	■																
m	Dolphin, Common	■																
m	Dolphin, Long-snouted Spinner	■																
m	Dolphin, Pantropical Spotted	■																
m	Dolphin, Risso's	■																
m	Dolphin, Striped	■																

GLOSSARY

Blackfish	General term for the larger members of the dolphin family.
Blowhole	The nostril of a cetacean, situated on the top of its head. Toothed whales have a single nostril whilst baleen whales have a double.
Bow-riding	Riding on the pressure wave created by the bow of a boat or the head of a large whale.
Breaching	See page 128.
Carapace	The shell of a tortoise or turtle.
Cere	The fleshy area at the base of the bill.
Cetacean	Generic term for the Order Cetacea which includes all of the whales, dolphins and porpoises.
Crepuscular	Active in the dim light of dusk and dawn.
Eclipse plumage	The dull plumage which briefly replaces the full adult breeding plumage each year; in the case of ducks, males acquire a female-type plumage.
Endemic	Restricted to a particular geographical region.
Falcate	Hooked or curved like a sickle.
Fluking	See page 128.
Frontal shield	Area of often brightly coloured bare skin on the forehead of a bird.
Gonydeal angle	The angle of the ridge formed by the junction of the two halves of a bird's lower mandible, near the tip of the bill.
Gular	Pertaining to the throat.
Hirundine	A member of the swallow and martin family.
Inshore	Close to shore.
Kleptoparasite	An individual that forcibly steals food items obtained by another individual, often through violent harassment for prolonged periods.
Lobtailing	Common behaviour in cetaceans when the tail fluke is lifted out of the water and slapped powerfully down on the surface.
Logging	See page 129.
Melon	Bulbous-shaped forehead on a cetacean.
Migrant	A species that undertakes periodic movements to and from a given area, usually along well-defined routes and at predictable times of the year.
Offshore	Some distance from shore.
Passerine	A member of the Order Passeriformes – generally small perching birds with the large first toe pointing backwards and the outer three toes forward.
Pelagic	Term used to descibe a species that spends all or most of its life at sea.
Plastron	The hard plate which forms the underside of a tortoise or turtle.
Pod	A co-ordinated group of cetaceans. Generally used only in reference to the toothed cetaceans.
Porpoising	See page 129.
Resident	Remaining throughout the year in a given area.
Spy-hopping	See page 128.
Subspecies	A population of a species which differs in size and/or appearance from other populations of the same species (also known as a 'race').
Vagrant	An individual that wanders outside the normal range of the species.

FURTHER READING

Bowman, R.I., Berson, M. and Leviton, A.E. (eds) 1983. Patterns of Evolution in Galápagos Organisms. American Association for the Advancement of Science, Pacific Division, San Francisco, USA.

Burghardt, G.M. and Rand, A.S. (eds) 1983. Iguanas of the World: Their Behavior, Ecology, and Conservation. Noyes Publications, New Jersey, USA.

Carwardine, M. 1995. Whales, Dolphins and Porpoises: the visual guide to all the world's cetaceans. Dorling Kindersley, London, UK.

Castro, I. and Phillips, A. 1996. A Guide to the Birds of the Galápagos Islands. Christopher Helm/A & C Black, London, UK.

Cepeda, F. and Cruz, J.B. 1994. Status and management of seabirds on the Galápagos Islands, Ecuador. Pp 268-278 in D.N. Nettleship, J. Burger and M. Gochfeld (eds). Seabirds on islands: threats, case studies and action plans. BirdLife Conservation Series No. 1. BirdLife International, Cambridge, UK.

Clark, D.B. 1980. Population ecology of an endemic neotropical island rodent Oryzomys bauri of Santa Fé Island, Galápagos. J. Animal Ecology 49:185–198.

Collar, N.J., Gonzaga, L.P., Krabbe, N., Madroño Nieto, A., Naranjo, L.G., Parker T.A. and Wege, D.C. 1992. Threatened Birds of the Americas: the ICBP/IUCN Red Data Book. International Council for Bird Preservation, Cambridge, UK.

Constant, P. 1995. The Galápagos Islands. Odyssey Illustrated Guide. The Guidebook Company, Hong Kong.

De Roy, T. 1998. Galápagos Islands Born of Fire. Airlife, England.

Grant, P.R. 1986 (1999). Ecology and Evolution of Darwin's Finches. Princeton University Press, New Jersey, USA.

Harris, M. 1974 (1982). A Field Guide to the Birds of Galápagos. Collins, London, UK.

Harrison, P. 1983 (1993). Seabirds: an identification guide. Croom Helm, Beckenham, UK.

Horwell, D. and Oxford, P. 1999. Galápagos Wildlife: a visitor's guide. Bradt Publications, UK.

Jackson, M.H. 1993. Galápagos, a natural history. University of Calgary Press, Canada.

Lack, D. 1947. Darwin's Finches. Cambridge University Press, UK.

Leatherwood, S., Evans, W.E. and Rice, D.W. 1972. The Whales, Dolphins and Porpoises of the Eastern North Pacific: A Guide to their Identification in the Water. Naval Undersea Research and Development Center, San Diego.

Marchant, J., Prater, T. and Hayman, P. 1986. Shorebirds: an identification guide to the waders of the world. Croom Helm, Beckenham, UK.

Perry, R. (ed) 1984. Key Environments: Galapagos. Pergamon Press, Oxford, UK.

Pritchard, P.C.H. 1996. The Galapagos Tortoises: Nomenclature and Survival Status. Chelonian Research Monographs No. 1. Chelonian Research Foundation, Lunenberg, Massachusetts, USA.

Steadman, D.W. and Zousmer, S. 1988. Galápagos: Discovery on Darwin's Islands. Airlife, England.

Weiner, J. 1994. The Beak of the Finch: A History of Evolution in Our Time. Alfred A. Knopf, New York, USA.

ELECTRONIC MEDIA

Galapágos Conservancy
http://www.galapagos.org

Charles Darwin Foundation
http://www.darwinfoundation.org

Fundación Galápagos
http://www.fundaciongalapagos.org

Galápagos Conservation Trust
http://www.gct.org

Galápagos Geology on the Web
http://www.geo.cornell.edu/geology/GalapagosWWW/GalapagosGeology.html

CONTACT ADDRESSES

Galápagos Conservancy
407 North Washington Street, Suite 105, Falls Church, VA 22046-3436, USA.
Tel: (703) 538 6833; Fax: (703) 538 6835
Email: comments@galapagos.org

Charles Darwin Foundation for the Galápagos Islands
Av. 6 de Diciembre N 36-109 y Pasaje California, Post Box 17-01-3891, Quito, Ecuador. Tel: (593) 2 224 4803;
Fax: (593) 2 244 3935
Email: cdrs@fcdarwin.org.ec

Charles Darwin Research Station (CDRS)
Puerto Ayora, Santa Cruz, Galápagos Islands, Ecuador. Tel: (593) 5 2526 146/147;
Fax: (593) 5 2526 146/147 Ext 102
Email: cdrs@fcdarwin.org.ec

Galápagos Conservation Trust (GCT)
5 Derby Street, London W1J 7AB, UK.
Tel: (0)20 7629 5049; Fax: (0)20 7629 4149
Email: gct@gct.org

PHOTOGRAPHIC AND ARTWORK CREDITS

Each of the photographs and illustrations used in this book is listed in this section. As much information as possible is given, including, where known, details of the location and date, as well as the name of the photographer or artist.

The habitats of the Galápagos

Page 12. **Seabird feeding frenzy:** off Roca Redonda; August 1995; Andy Swash.

Page 12. **Rocky islet:** Roca Redonda; August 1995; Andy Swash.

Page 13. **Seabird colony:** Genovesa; January 1996; Andy Swash.

Page 13. **Rocky shore:** Fernandina; August 1995; Andy Swash.

Page 13. **Sandy beach and mangroves:** Black Beach, Isabela; August 1995; Andy Swash.

Page 14. **Mangroves:** Turtle Cove, Santa Cruz; August 1995; Andy Swash.

Page 14. **Lagoon bordered by Saltbush:** Rábida; January 1996; Andy Swash.

Page 14. **Prickly Pear Opuntia cacti and Sea Purslane Sesuvium:** South Plaza, August 1995; Andy Swash.

Page 15. **Palo Santo zone, dry season:** Darwin's Lagoon, Isabela; August 1995; Andy Swash.

Page 15. **Transition zone, agricultural area:** Santa Cruz; August 1995; Andy Swash.

Page 15. **Transition zone, disused agricultural area:** Floreana; August 1995; Andy Swash.

Page 16. **Scalesia zone:** Santa Cruz; January 1996; Andy Swash.

Page 16. **Pampa zone:** Isabela; January 1996; Andy Swash.

The birds of the Galápagos

Page 18. **Swallow-tailed Gull:** Adult, in flight; South Plaza, Galápagos; August 1995; Andy Swash.

Page 18. **Semipalmated Plover:** Adult; Jamaica Bay, New York, USA; August; Arthur Morris (Windrush).

Page 18. **Large Ground Finch:** Adult female; Genovesa, Galápagos; January 1996; Andy Swash.

Page 18. **Chatham Mockingbird:** Adult, on branch; San Cristóbal, Galápagos; August 1995; Andy Swash.

Page 20. **Galápagos Penguin:** Adult; Bartolomé, Galápagos; August 1995; Andy Swash.

Page 21. **Flightless (or Galápagos) Cormorant:** Adult; Isabela, Galápagos; August 1995; Andy Swash.

Page 21. **Brown Pelican:** Adult; Fernandina, Galápagos; August 1995; Andy Swash.

Page 21. **Waved Albatross:** Adult; Española, Galápagos; August 1995; Andy Swash.

Page 21. **Galápagos Shearwater:** Adult; at sea off Roca Redonda, Galápagos; August 1995; Andy Swash.

Page 22. **Dark-rumped Petrel:** Adult; at sea off Isabela, Galápagos; August 1995; Andy Swash.

Page 22. **Elliot's Storm-petrel:** Adult; off Roca Redonda, Galápagos; August 1995; Andy Swash.

Page 22. **Magnificent Frigatebird:** Adult male; North Seymour, Galápagos; August 1995; Andy Swash.

Page 22. **Nazca Booby:** Adult; Genovesa, Galápagos; August 1995; Andy Swash.

Page 23. **South Polar Skua:** Adult, in flight; Half Moon Island, Antarctica; January 1993; John Cooper.

Page 23. **Swallow-tailed Gull:** Adult and chick; Genovesa, Galápagos; January 1996; Andy Swash.

Page 23. **Common Noddy:** Adult; Michaelmas Cay, Great Barrier Reef, Queensland, Australia; September 1989; Andy Swash.

Page 23. **Red-billed Tropicbird:** Adult; South Plaza, Galápagos; August 1995; Andy Swash.

Page 24. **Pied-billed Grebe:** Adult; Sanibel Island, Florida, USA; April 1989; Gordon Langsbury.

Page 24. **White-cheeked Pintail:** Adults; Santa Cruz, Galápagos; August 1995; Andy Swash.

Page 24. **Galápagos Rail:** Adult; Isabela, Galápagos; August 1995; Andy Swash.

Page 25. **Greater Flamingo:** Adults; Floreana, Galápagos; May 1997; Bruce Hallett.

Page 25. **Lava (or Galápagos) Heron:** Adult; Santiago, Galápagos; August 1995; Andy Swash.

Page 25. **American Oystercatcher:** Adult; Fernandina, Galápagos; August 1995; Andy Swash.

Page 26. **Black-necked Stilt:** Adults; Chomes, Costa Rica; February 1994; Andy Swash.

Page 26. **Semipalmated Plover:** Adult, non-breeding; North Seymour, Galápagos; August 1995; Andy Swash.

Page 26. **Black-bellied (or Grey) Plover:** Juvenile; Zach's Bay, New York, USA; October 1986; Arthur Morris (Windrush).

Page 26. **Whimbrel:** Adult; Chomes, Costa Rica; February 1991; Andy Swash.

Page 26. **Wandering Tattler:** Adult; Isabela, Galápagos; August 1995; Andy Swash.

Page 26. **Red-necked Phalarope:** Juvenile; Cornwall, UK; September 1993; Andy Swash.

Page 27. **Osprey:** Juvenile; Fort Myers Beach, Florida, USA; May 1998; Gordon Langsbury.

Page 27. **Galápagos Hawk:** Immature; Santiago, Galápagos; August 1995; Andy Swash.

Page 27. **Peregrine:** Adult; West Sussex, UK; June 1998; Gordon Langsbury.

Page 28. **Barn Owl:** Adult, illustration by Ian Lewington.

Page 28. **Short-eared Owl:** Adult; Santa Cruz, Galápagos; August 1995; Andy Swash.

Page 28. **Common Nighthawk:** Adult male; Texas, USA; April 1989; Andy Swash.

Page 29. **Galápagos Dove:** Adult; Genovesa, Galápagos; January 1996; Andy Swash.

Page 29. **Belted Kingfisher:** Adult female; Jamaica Bay, New York, USA; August; Arthur Morris (Windrush).

Page 29. **Dark-billed Cuckoo:** Adult; Palomitas, Argentina; February 1995; John Cooper.

Page 30. **Chimney Swift:** Illustration by Ian Lewington.

Page 30. **Galápagos Martin:** Adult male; illustration by Ian Lewington.

Page 31. **Vermilion Flycatcher:** Adult male; Santa Cruz, Galápagos; August 1995; Andy Swash.

Page 31. **Yellow Warbler:** Adult male; Santa Fé, Galápagos; August 1995; Andy Swash.

Page 31. **Red-eyed Vireo:** Adult; Point Pelee, Ontario, Canada; May; Arthur Morris (Windrush).

Page 31. **Bananaquit:** Adult; Trinidad; April 1998; Yvonne Dean.

Page 31. **Cedar Waxwing:** Adult; Riding Mountain NP, Manitoba, Canada; June 1997; Brayton Holt.

Page 31. **Rose-breasted Grosbeak:** Adult female; Ontario, Canada; May; Arthur Morris (Windrush).

Page 32. **Summer Tanager:** Adult female; La Selva, Costa Rica; February 1991; Andy Swash.

Page 32. **Bobolink:** Juvenile; Devon, UK; September 1991; David Tipling (Windrush).

157

Page 32. **Galápagos Mockingbird:** Adult; Genovesa, Galápagos; January 1996; Andy Swash.
Page 32. **Small Ground Finch:** Adult male; Santa Cruz, Galápagos; August 1995; Andy Swash.
Page 32. **Warbler Finch:** Adult; Santa Cruz, Galápagos; August 1995; Andy Swash.

The bird plates

All the photographs used in the plates are listed in this section; the species are listed in alphabetical order:

Plate 1

Brown Pelican: Adult; Rábida, Galápagos; August 1995; Andy Swash.
Brown Pelican: Chick; Rábida, Galápagos; August 1995; Andy Swash.
Brown Pelican: Juvenile in flight; Santa Cruz, Galápagos; August 1995; Andy Swash.
Brown Pelican: Juvenile; Santa Cruz, Galápagos; August 1995; Andy Swash.
Flightless (or Galápagos) Cormorant: Adult; Isabela, Galápagos; August 1995; Andy Swash.
Galápagos Penguin: Adult; Tagus Cove, Isabela, Galápagos; August 1995; Andy Swash.
Galápagos Penguin: Juvenile; Isabela, Galápagos; August 1995; Philip Newbold.

Plate 2

Black-browed Albatross: Adult, in flight showing upperside; at sea off Argentina; January 1994; Andy Swash.
Black-browed Albatross: Adult, in flight showing underside; at sea off Argentina; January 1994; Andy Swash.
Black-browed Albatross: Immature in flight; at sea off Argentina; January 1994; Andy Swash.
Black-footed Albatross: Adult, in flight; Midway Island; March 1997; Roger Charlwood.
Royal Albatross: Subadult, in flight; off Campbell Island; January 1994; Tony Palliser.
Southern Giant Petrel: Adult, in flight showing underside; Beagle Channel, Argentina; January 1994; Andy Swash.
Southern Giant Petrel: Adult, in flight showing upperside; Beagle Channel, Argentina; January 1994; Andy Swash.
Wandering Albatross: Adult, in flight; off Sydney, New South Wales, Australia; October 1998; Tony Palliser.
Waved Albatross: Adult, in flight showing upperside; Española, Galápagos; August 1995; Andy Swash.
Waved Albatross: Adult, in flight showing underside; Española, Galápagos; August 1995; Andy Swash.
Waved Albatross: Adult; Española, Galápagos; August 1995; Andy Swash.
Waved Albatross: Chick; Española, Galápagos; November 1994; Ralph Todd (Windrush).

Plate 3

Galápagos Shearwater: Adult, in flight showing upperside; Baltra, Galápagos; August 1995; Andy Swash.
Galápagos Shearwater: Adult, in flight showing underside; Baltra, Galápagos; August 1995; Andy Swash.
Galápagos Shearwater: Adults on water; off Española, Galápagos; August 1995; Andy Swash.
Parkinson's Black Petrel: Adult, in flight; off Sydney, New South Wales, Australia; December 1997; Dick Newell.
Pink-footed Shearwater: Adult, in flight from above; off Quintero, Chile; November 2003; Andy Swash.
Pink-footed Shearwater: Adult, in flight; at sea off Chile; November 1992; Roger Charlwood.
Sooty Shearwater: Adult, in flight showing upperside; at sea off Argentina; January 1994; Andy Swash.
Sooty Shearwater: Adult, in flight showing underside; at sea off Argentina; January 1994; Andy Swash.

Wedge-tailed Shearwater: Adult, pale morph, in flight (digitally manipulated image of dark morph); at sea off Sydney, New South Wales, Australia; Tony Palliser.

Plate 4

Antarctic Prion: Adult, in flight; Macquarie Island; January 1998; Hadoram Shirihai.
Cape Petrel: Adult, in flight; at sea, Antarctica; January 1994; Andy Swash.
Dark-rumped Petrel: Adult, in flight showing upperside; at sea off Isabela, Galápagos; August 1995; Andy Swash.
Dark-rumped Petrel: Adult, in flight showing underside; at sea off Isabela, Galápagos; August 1995; Andy Swash.
Gould's (or White-winged) Petrel: Adult, in flight; Central Pacific Ocean; December 1988; Mark Rauzon.
Mottled Petrel: Adult, in flight; illustration by Ian Lewington.
Southern Fulmar: Adult, in flight; at sea, Antarctica; January 1994; Andy Swash.

Plate 5

Elliot's Storm-petrel: Adults, in flight; off Roca Redonda, Galápagos; August 1995; Andy Swash.
Elliot's Storm-petrel: Adult, in flight showing underside; Galápagos; August 1997; Paul Ellis.
Madeiran Storm-petrel: Adult, in flight; off Isabela, Galápagos; December 1999; David Tipling (Windrush).
Wedge-rumped Storm-petrel: Adult, in flight; off Roca Redonda, Galápagos; August 1995; Andy Swash.

Plate 6

Black Storm-petrel: Adult, in flight; illustration by Ian Lewington.
Leach's Storm-petrel: Adult, in flight showing upperside; Blackpool, Lancashire, UK; September 1987; Steve Young.
Leach's Storm-petrel: Adult, in flight showing underside; Blackpool, Lancashire, UK; September 1987; Steve Young.
Markham's Storm-petrel: Adult, in flight; illustration by Ian Lewington.
White-bellied Storm-petrel: Digitally manipulated image of adult Black-bellied Storm-petrel in flight showing underside; off Sydney, New South Wales, Australia; December 1995; Tony Palliser.
White-faced Storm-petrel: Adult, in flight; off Sydney, New South Wales, Australia; September 1996; Tony Palliser.

Plate 7

Great Frigatebird: Adult female; Genovesa, Galápagos; January 1996; Andy Swash.
Great Frigatebird: Adult female, in flight; Jarvis Island, Central Pacific; April 1990; Mark Rauzon.
Great Frigatebird: Adult male; Genovesa, Galápagos; January 1996; Andy Swash.
Great Frigatebird: Juvenile; Genovesa, Galápagos; January 1996; Andy Swash.
Great Frigatebird: Juvenile, in flight; Genovesa, Galápagos; January 1996; Andy Swash.
Magnificent Frigatebird: Adult female; North Seymour, Galápagos; August 1995; Andy Swash.
Magnificent Frigatebird: Adult female, in flight; Galápagos; Howard Nicholls (Windrush).
Magnificent Frigatebird: Adult male; North Seymour, Galápagos; August 1995; Andy Swash.
Magnificent Frigatebird: Adult male, in flight; Marco Island, Florida, USA; Arthur Morris (Windrush).
Magnificent Frigatebird: Juvenile; North Seymour, Galápagos; November 1994; Ralph Todd.
Magnificent Frigatebird: Juvenile, in flight; Florida, USA; April 1993; Gordon Langsbury (Windrush).

Plate 8
Blue-footed Booby: Adult; North Seymour, Galápagos; August 1995; Andy Swash.
Blue-footed Booby: Adult, in flight; Baltra Harbour, Galápagos; August 1997; Phil Hansbro.
Blue-footed Booby: Juvenile; San Cristóbal, Galápagos; August 1995; Andy Swash.
Brown Booby: Adult, in flight; San Salvador, Bahamas; May 1995; Bruce Hallett.
Nazca Booby: Adult; Genovesa, Galápagos; January 1996; Andy Swash.
Nazca Booby: Adult, in flight showing underside; Daphne Major, Galápagos; January 1996; Andy Swash.
Nazca Booby: Adult, in flight showing upperside; Española, Galápagos; May 1997; Bruce Hallett.
Nazca Booby: Juvenile; Genovesa, Galápagos; August 1995; Andy Swash.
Red-footed Booby: Adult, brown form; Genovesa, Galápagos; August 1995; Andy Swash.
Red-footed Booby: Adult, white form; Genovesa, Galápagos; August 1995; Andy Swash.
Red-footed Booby: Adult, brown form, in flight; Genovesa, Galápagos; November 1994; Ralph Todd.
Red-footed Booby: Adult, white form, in flight; Kevin Carlson (Windrush).
Red-footed Booby: Juvenile; Genovesa, Galápagos; August 1995; Andy Swash.

Plate 9
Lava Gull: Adult; North Seymour, Galápagos; August 1995; Andy Swash.
Lava Gull: First-winter, in flight; Galápagos; December 1987; Alan Tate.
Lava Gull: Juvenile; Isabela, Galápagos; August 1995; Andy Swash.
Pomarine Jaeger/Skua: Adult, non-breeding, pale phase, in flight; off Senegal; October 1995; Dick Newell.
Pomarine Jaeger/Skua: Adult, breeding, pale phase, in flight; Taymyr, Russia; July 1994; Brayton Holt.
Pomarine Jaeger/Skua: Juvenile; Fleetwood, Lancashire, UK; April 1995; Steve Young.
Pomarine Jaeger/Skua: Juvenile, in flight; off St Simon's Island, Georgia, USA; October 1997; Giff Beaton.
South Polar Skua: Adult, in flight; Half Moon Island, Antarctica; January 1993; John Cooper.
Swallow-tailed Gull: Adult; Genovesa, Galápagos; January 1996; Andy Swash.
Swallow-tailed Gull: Adult, in flight; South Plaza, Galápagos; August 1995; Andy Swash.
Swallow-tailed Gull: Juvenile; Genovesa, Galápagos; August 1995; Andy Swash.

Plate 10
Franklin's Gull: Adult, breeding, in flight; Benton Lakes, Montana, USA; June; Arthur Morris (Windrush).
Franklin's Gull: Adult, non-breeding; Namibia; February 1999; Alan Tate.
Franklin's Gull: First-winter; Tempisque River, Costa Rica; February 1996; Andy Swash.
Grey-headed Gull: Adult breeding; Velddrif, South Africa; October 1997; Andy Swash.
Kelp Gull: Adult, breeding; Lambert's Bay, South Africa; October 1997; Andy Swash.
Kelp Gull: Adult, breeding, in flight; Dunedin; October 1996; Phil Hansbro.
Kelp Gull: First-winter; Chile; February 1990; Alan Tate.
Kelp Gull: First-winter, in flight; Chatham Island; October 1996; Phil Hansbro.
Kelp Gull: Second-summer; Chile; November 1992; Roger Charlwood.

Laughing Gull: Adult, breeding; Florida, USA; March 1987; Andy Swash.
Laughing Gull: Adult, breeding, in flight; Galveston Texas, USA; April 1993; Gordon Langsbury.
Laughing Gull: Adult, non-breeding; Sanibel Island, Florida, USA; December 1994; Gordon Langsbury.
Laughing Gull: First-winter; Tempisque River, Costa Rica; February 1996; Andy Swash.
Laughing Gull: First-winter, in flight; Tempisque River, Costa Rica; February 1996; Andy Swash.

Plate 11
Common Noddy: Adult; Michaelmas Cay, Great Barrier Reef, Queensland, Australia; October 1989; Andy Swash.
Common Noddy: Adult, in flight; Dry Tortugas, Florida, USA; April 1991; Gordon Langsbury.
Red-billed Tropicbird: Adult, in flight, South Plaza, Galápagos; August 1995; Andy Swash.
Sooty Tern: Adult; Michaelmas Cay, Great Barrier Reef, Queensland, Australia; October 1989; Andy Swash.
Sooty Tern: Adult, in flight; Michaelmas Cay, Great Barrier Reef, Queensland, Australia; October 1989; Andy Swash.
Sooty Tern: Juvenile; Michaelmas Cay, Great Barrier Reef, Queensland, Australia; October 1989; Andy Swash.

Plate 12
Black Tern: Adult, breeding; Seaforth, Merseyside, UK; May 1997; Steve Young.
Black Tern: Adult, non-breeding, moulting, in flight; Crosby, Merseyside, UK; September 1994; Steve Young.
Black Tern: First-winter; Gambia; February; Barry Hughes (Windrush).
Common Tern: Adult, breeding, in flight; Fort Myers Beach, Florida, USA; April 1989; Gordon Langsbury.
Common Tern: Adult, breeding; Great Gull Island, New York, USA; June; Arthur Morris (Windrush).
Common Tern: First-winter; Kommetjie, South Africa; October 1997; Andy Swash.
Royal Tern: Adult, non-breeding; Florida, USA; January 1990; Paul Doherty.
Royal Tern: Adult, non-breeding, in flight; Florida, USA; October 1988; Paul Doherty.
White Tern: Adult, in flight; South Pacific; March; Alan Tate.

Plate 13
American Coot: Adult; Brazos Bend, Texas, USA; February 1995; Andy Swash.
Black-bellied Whistling Duck: Adult; Texas, USA; A & E Morris (Windrush).
Blue-winged Teal: Adult male and female, breeding; Florida, USA; March; David Tipling (Windrush).
Masked Duck: Adult female; Brazos Bend, Texas, USA; February 1995; Andy Swash.
Masked Duck: Adult male; Brazos Bend, Texas, USA; February 1995; Andy Swash.
Pied-billed Grebe: Adult; Sanibel Island, Florida, USA; April 1989; Gordon Langsbury.
White-cheeked (or Galápagos) Pintail: Adult; Santa Cruz, Galápagos; August 1995; Andy Swash.

Plate 14
American Purple Gallinule: Adult; Brazos Bend, Texas, USA; April 1993; Gordon Langsbury.
American Purple Gallinule: Juvenile; Loxahatchee NWR, Florida, USA; February 1995; Giff Beaton.
Common Gallinule (or Moorhen): Adult; Florida, USA; April 1988; Gordon Langsbury.
Common Gallinule (or Moorhen): Juvenile; Lake Woodruff NWR, Florida USA; Arthur Morris (Windrush).
Galápagos Rail: Adult; Isabela, Galápagos; August 1995; Philip Newbold.

Paint-billed Crake: Adult; illustration by Ian Lewington.
Sora (Rail): Adult, breeding; Merritt Island, Florida, USA; April 1998; Gordon Langsbury.
Sora (Rail): Immature; Texas, USA; January 1995; Andy Swash.

Plate 15
Great Blue Heron: Adult; Lake Okeechobee, Florida, USA; March 1990; Rob Still.
Great Blue Heron: Juvenile; Santa Cruz, Galápagos; August 1995; Andy Swash.
Greater Flamingo: Adult; Isabela, Galápagos; August 1995; Andy Swash.
Greater Flamingo: Adults in flight; Eilat, Israel; July 1988; Hadoram Shirihai. Digitally manipulated.
Greater Flamingo: Immature, feeding; Coto Doñana, Spain; April 1992; Andy Swash.
Little Blue Heron: Adult; Florida, USA; April 1987; Andy Swash.
Tricolored Heron: Adult; Florida, USA; February 1994; Andy Swash.

Plate 16
Cattle Egret: Adult, breeding; Florida, USA; April 1987; Andy Swash.
Cattle Egret: Adult, non-breeding; Israel; December 1997; Dave Nye.
Great Egret: Adult; The Gambia; January 1991; Gordon Langsbury.
Little Blue Heron: Juvenile; Florida, USA; February 1994; Andy Swash.
Snowy Egret: Adult, breeding; Florida, USA; April 1987; Andy Swash.

Plate 17
Black-crowned Night-heron: Adult; The Gambia; John Geeson.
Black-crowned Night-heron: Juvenile; Costanera Sur, Argentina ; January 1993; Andy Swash.
Green Heron: Adult; Hato Piñero, Venezuela; February 1992; Andy Swash.
Lava (or Galápagos) Heron: Adult breeding; Florida, USA; February 1994; Andy Swash.
Lava (or Galápagos) Heron: Juvenile; Fernandina, Galápagos; August 1995; Andy Swash.
Striated Heron: Adult; Hato Piñero, Venezuela; February 1992; Andy Swash.
Striated Heron: Juvenile; South Sanai, Israel; February 1987; Hadoram Shirihai.
Yellow-crowned Night-heron: Adult; Genovesa, Galápagos; January 1996; Andy Swash.
Yellow-crowned Night-heron: Immature; Genovesa, Galápagos; May 1997; Bruce Hallett.
Yellow-crowned Night-heron: Juvenile; Arthur Morris (Windrush).

Plate 18
American Oystercatcher: Adult; Fernandina, Galápagos; August 1995; Andy Swash.
American Oystercatcher: Adult, in flight; Florida, USA; September 1988; Paul Doherty.
Black Turnstone: Adult, breeding; California, USA; April 1987; Andy Swash.
Black-necked Stilt: Adult; Chomes, Costa Rica; February 1991; Andy Swash.
Black-necked Stilt: Adult, in flight; Salton Sea, California, USA; Arthur Morris (Windrush).
Ruddy Turnstone: Adult male, breeding; Sanibel Island, Florida, USA; April 1998; Gordon Langsbury.
Ruddy Turnstone: Juvenile; The Netherlands; October 1997; Gordon Langsbury.

Ruddy Turnstone: Juvenile moulting into first-winter, in flight; Kent, UK; November 1990; Paul Doherty.
Surfbird: Adult, breeding; California, USA; April 1987; Andy Swash.

Plate 19
American Golden Plover: Adult, breeding; Churchill, Manitoba, Canada; June; Arthur Morris (Windrush).
American Golden Plover: Juvenile; UK; October; David Tipling (Windrush).
Black-bellied (or Grey) Plover: Juvenile; Zach's Bay, New York, USA; October 1986; Arthur Morris (Windrush).
Black-bellied (or Grey) Plover: Adult, breeding; Richard Revels (Windrush).
Killdeer: Adult, non-breeding; Sanibel Island, Florida, USA; December 1994; Gordon Langsbury.
Pacific Golden Plover: Juvenile, moulting; Hawaii; December; A & E Morris (Windrush).
Semipalmated Plover: Adult; Jamaica Bay, New York, USA; August; Arthur Morris (Windrush).
Semipalmated Plover: Adult, non-breeding; Fort Myers Beach, Florida, USA; December 1994; Gordon Langsbury.
Wilson's Plover: Adult female, breeding; Fort Myers Beach, Florida, USA; Arthur Morris (Windrush).
Wilson's Plover: Adult male, breeding; Fort Myers Beach, Florida, USA; April 1988; Gordon Langsbury.

Plate 20
Hudsonian Godwit: Adult, breeding; Churchill, Manitoba, USA; June; Arthur Morris (Windrush).
Hudsonian Godwit: Adult, non-breeding; USA; Arthur Morris (Windrush).
Marbled Godwit: Adult; San Diego, California, USA; February 1988; Arthur Morris (Windrush).
Marbled Godwit: Juvenile, in flight; Florida, USA; October 1988; Paul Doherty.
Short-billed Dowitcher: Adult, breeding; Churchill, Manitoba, Canada; June 1997; Brayton Holt.
Short-billed Dowitcher: Adult, moulting; Fort Myers Beach, Florida, USA; April 1991; Gordon Langsbury.
Short-billed Dowitcher: Adult, non-breeding, in flight; Florida, USA; January 1990; Paul Doherty.
Whimbrel: Adult; Chomes, Costa Rica; February 1991; Andy Swash.
Whimbrel: Adult, in flight; Florida, USA; September 1988; Paul Doherty.
Willet: Adult, breeding; Texas, USA; April 1989; Andy Swash.
Willet: Adult, non-breeding; Texas, USA; January 1995; Andy Swash.
Willet: Adult, in flight; Florida, USA; April 1987; Andy Swash.

Plate 21
Buff-breasted Sandpiper: Juvenile; Tacumshin, County Wexford, Ireland; August 1994; Tom Ennis (Windrush).
Greater Yellowlegs: Adult, breeding; Fort Myers Beach, Florida, USA; April 1995; Gordon Langsbury.
Greater Yellowlegs: First-winter; Bosque del Apache, New Mexico, USA; January 1999; Gordon Langsbury.
Lesser Yellowlegs: Adult summer; Merritt Island, Florida, USA; Arthur Morris (Windrush).
Pectoral Sandpiper: Adult female, breeding; Norfolk, UK; June; Tim Loseby.
Stilt Sandpiper: Adult summer; Cambridge Bay, Canada; July 1997; Chris Schenk (Windrush).
Stilt Sandpiper: Juvenile; Jamaica Bay, New York, USA; August; Arthur Morris (Windrush).

Plate 22
Red Knot: Adult, breeding; Fort Myers Beach, Florida, USA; May 1989; Gordon Langsbury.

Red Knot: Adult, non-breeding; Fort Myers Beach, Florida, USA; April 1991; Gordon Langsbury.

Sanderling: Adult summer; Cook's Beach, Jew Jersey, USA; A & E Morris (Windrush).

Sanderling: Adult, non-breeding; Isles of Scilly, UK; October 1993; Andy Swash.

Solitary Sandpiper: Adult, breeding; Merritt Island, Florida, USA; April 1998; Gordon Langsbury.

Spotted Sandpiper: Adult, breeding; Merritt Island, Florida, USA; April 1998; Gordon Langsbury.

Spotted Sandpiper: Juvenile; Sanibel Island, Florida, USA; December 1994; Gordon Langsbury.

Wandering Tattler: Adult, breeding; Isabela, Galápagos; August 1995; Andy Swash.

Wandering Tattler: Juvenile; Green Island, Queensland, Australia; October 1989; Andy Swash.

Plate 23

Baird's Sandpiper: Adult, non-breeding; Ushuaia, Argentina; January 1993; Brayton Holt.

Baird's Sandpiper: Juvenile; Jamaica Bay, New York, USA; August; Arthur Morris (Windrush).

Least Sandpiper: Adult, breeding; Sanibel Island, Florida, USA; April 1988; Gordon Langsbury.

Least Sandpiper: Worn adult; Jamaica Bay, New York, USA; August; Arthur Morris (Windrush).

Semipalmated Sandpiper: Adult, non-breeding; Fort Myers Beach, Florida, USA; April 1989; Gordon Langsbury.

Semipalmated Sandpiper: Juvenile; Jamaica Bay, New York, USA; August; Arthur Morris (Windrush).

Western Sandpiper: Adult, non-breeding; Fort Myers Beach, Florida, USA; April 1991; Gordon Langsbury.

Western Sandpiper: Adult, non-breeding; Florida, USA; Arthur Morris (Windrush).

White-rumped Sandpiper: Adult, non-breeding; Falkland Islands; January 1993; Gordon Langsbury.

White-rumped Sandpiper: Juvenile; Madeira; October 1993; Andy Swash.

Plate 24

Red (or Grey) Phalarope: Adult female, breeding; Cambridge Bay, Canada; July 1997; Chris Schenk (Windrush).

Red (or Grey) Phalarope: Adult male, breeding; Captive, Pensthorpe Wildlife Park, UK; May 1994; Gordon Langsbury.

Red (or Grey) Phalarope: Adult, non-breeding,; Norfolk, UK; July 1993; Tim Loseby.

Red (or Grey) Phalarope: Juvenile, moulting; Angler's Country Park, Yorkshire, UK; September 1992; Paul Doherty.

Red-necked Phalarope: Adult female, breeding; Churchill, Manitoba, Canada; June; Arthur Morris (Windrush).

Red-necked Phalarope: Adult male, breeding; Fetlar, Shetland Islands, UK; June 1993; Gordon Langsbury.

Red-necked Phalarope: Adult, non-breeding; Salton Sea, California, USA; September 1993; Nigel Bean.

Red-necked and Red (or Grey) Phalaropes: Adults, non-breeding, in flight; off Isabela, Galápagos; August 1995; Andy Swash.

Red-necked Phalarope: Juvenile; Jamaica Bay, New York, USA; August; Arthur Morris (Windrush).

Wilson's Phalarope: Adult female, breeding; Montana, USA; Arthur Morris (Windrush).

Wilson's Phalarope: Adult, non-breeding; Cornwall, UK; August; David Tipling (Windrush).

Plate 25

Galápagos Hawk: Adult, in flight showing upperside; Española, Galápagos; November 1994; Ralph Todd.

Galápagos Hawk: Adult, in flight showing underside; Fernandina, Galápagos; August 1997; Phil Hansbro.

Galápagos Hawk: Immature; Santa Fé, Galápagos; August 1995; Andy Swash.

Galápagos Hawk: Juvenile; Santa Fé, Galápagos; August 1995; Andy Swash.

Osprey: Adult; Sanibel Island, Florida, USA; December 1994; Gordon Langsbury.

Osprey: Juvenile, in flight; Fort Myers Beach, Florida, USA; May 1998; Gordon Langsbury.

Peregrine: Adult female; Wales; May; Howard Nicholls (Windrush).

Peregrine: Adult, in flight; West Sussex, UK; June 1998; Gordon Langsbury.

Plate 26

Barn Owl: Adult; Baltra, Galápagos; November 1998; Ralph Todd.

Barn Owl: Adult, in flight; illustration by Ian Lewington.

Common Nighthawk: Adult male; Texas, USA; April 1989; Andy Swash.

Common Nighthawk: Adult male, in flight; Texas, USA; April 1989; Andy Swash.

Short-eared Owl: Adult; Santa Cruz, Galápagos; August 1995; Andy Swash.

Short-eared Owl: Adult, in flight; illustration by Ian Lewington.

Plate 27

Belted Kingfisher: Adult female; Jamaica Bay, New York; August; Arthur Morris (Windrush).

Belted Kingfisher: Adult male (digitally manipulated image of immature female); Bosque del Apache, New Mexico, USA; January 1998; Gordon Langsbury.

Eared Dove: Adult; J.V. Gonzales, Argentina; January 1993; Andy Swash.

Feral Pigeon: Adult; UK; February; David Tipling (Windrush).

Galápagos Dove: Adult; Genovesa, Galápagos; January 1996; Andy Swash.

Plate 28

Black-billed Cuckoo: Adult, on branch; Higbee's Beach, New Jersey, USA; Arthur Morris (Windrush).

Dark-billed Cuckoo: Adult; Palomitas, Argentina; February 1995; John Cooper.

Groove-billed Ani: Adult; La Selva, Costa Rica; February 1991; Andy Swash.

Smooth-billed Ani: Adult; Zapata Swamp, Cuba; March 2004; Andy Swash.

Plate 29

Bank Swallow (or Sand Martin); Barn Swallow; Chimney Swift; Cliff Swallow; Purple Martin and Galápagos Martin: illustrations by Ian Lewington.

Plate 30

Eastern Kingbird: Adult; Texas, USA; April 1989; Andy Swash.

Large-billed (or Galápagos) Flycatcher: Adult; Floreana, Galápagos; August 1995; Andy Swash.

Vermilion Flycatcher: Adult female; Floreana, Galápagos; August 1995; Andy Swash.

Vermilion Flycatcher: Adult male; Isabela, Galápagos; August 1995; Andy Swash.

Plate 31

Bananaquit: Adult; Trinidad; April 1998; Yvonne Dean.

Blackpoll Warbler: Adult male; Point Pelee, Ontario, Canada; May; A & E Morris (Windrush).

Blackpoll Warbler: Juvenile; Isles of Scilly, UK; October 1990; David Cottridge (Windrush).

Red-eyed Vireo: Adult; Point Pelee, Ontario, Canada; May; Arthur Morris (Windrush).
Yellow Warbler: Juvenile male; Genovesa, Galápagos; August 1995; Andy Swash.
Yellow Warbler: Adult male; Santa Fé, Galápagos; August 1995; Andy Swash.
Yellow Warbler: Immature; Isabela, Galápagos; May 1997; Bruce Hallett.

Plate 32
Bobolink: Adult male; Canada; Kevin Carlson (Windrush).
Bobolink: Juvenile; Devon, UK; September 1991; David Tipling (Windrush).
Cedar Waxwing: Adult; Riding Mountain NP, Manitoba, Canada; June 1997; Brayton Holt.
Indigo Bunting: Adult male; Point Pelee, Ontario, Canada; May; A & E Morris (Windrush).
Indigo Bunting: First-winter; Ramsey Island, Wales, UK; October 1996; Alan Tate.
Rose-breasted Grosbeak: Adult female; Ontario, Canada; May; Arthur Morris (Windrush).
Rose-breasted Grosbeak: Adult male; Ontario, Canada; May; Arthur Morris (Windrush).
Summer Tanager: Adult female; La Selva, Costa Rica; February 1991; Andy Swash.
Summer Tanager: Adult male; Big Bend NP, Texas, USA; May; Arthur Morris (Windrush).

Plate 33
Charles (or Floreana) Mockingbird: Adult; Champion, Galápagos; Heidi Snell.
Chatham (or San Cristóbal) Mockingbird: Adult; San Cristóbal, Galápagos; August 1995; Andy Swash.
Galápagos Mockingbird: Adult; Genovesa, Galápagos; January 1996; Andy Swash.
Hood Mockingbird: Adult; Española, Galápagos; August 1995; Andy Swash.

Plate 34
Darwin's Finches bills; measured drawings by Ian Lewington with photographs overlaid digitally. Based on specimens from The Natural History Museum, Tring, UK (the locality from which each specimen was taken is shown in brackets): Large Ground Finch (Genovesa); Medium Ground Finch (Santa Cruz); Small Ground Finch (San Cristóbal); Sharp-beaked Ground Finch (Wolf); Woodpecker Finch (Santa Cruz); Warbler Finch (Santa Cruz); Large Cactus Finch (*conirostris*) (Española); Large Cactus Finch (*propinqua*) (Genovesa); Cactus Finch (Floreana); Vegetarian Finch (Pinta); Large Tree Finch (Floreana); Medium Tree Finch (Floreana); and Small Tree Finch (San Cristóbal). The Mangrove Finch is drawn from a photograph taken by Andy Swash at Caleta Black, Isabela, Galápagos in August 1995.

Plate 35
Large Ground Finch: Adult male; Genovesa, Galápagos; January 1996; Andy Swash.
Large Ground Finch: Female; Genovesa, Galápagos; August 1995; Andy Swash.
Medium Ground Finch: Adult Male; Santa Cruz, Galápagos; December 1998; Heidi Snell.
Medium Ground Finch: Female; Santa Cruz, Galápagos; August 1995; Andy Swash.
Sharp-beaked Ground Finch: Adult male; Genovesa, Galápagos; August 1995; Andy Swash.
Sharp-beaked Ground Finch: Female; Genovesa, Galápagos; August 1995; Andy Swash.
Small Ground Finch: Adult male; Santa Cruz, Galápagos; August 1995; Andy Swash.
Small Ground Finch: Female; Santa Cruz, Galápagos; August 1995; Andy Swash.

Plate 36
Cactus Finch: Female; South Plaza, Galápagos; January 1996; Andy Swash.
Cactus Finch: Adult male; South Plaza, Galápagos; August 1995; Andy Swash.
Large Cactus Finch: Adult male ssp. *conirostris*; Española, Galápagos; August 1995; Andy Swash.
Large Cactus Finch: Female ssp. *conirostris*; Española, Galápagos; January 1996; Andy Swash.
Large Cactus Finch: Female ssp. *propinqua*; Genovesa, Galápagos; January 1996; Andy Swash.

Plate 37
Large Tree Finch: Adult male; Isabela, Galápagos; August 1995; Andy Swash.
Medium Tree Finch: Female/immature; Floreana, Galápagos; Windrush.
Small Tree Finch: Adult male; Santa Cruz, Galápagos; August 1995; Andy Swash.
Small Tree Finch: Female/immature; Floreana, Galápagos; August 1995; Andy Swash.
Vegetarian Finch: Adult; Galápagos; Michael Gore (Windrush).

Plate 38
Mangrove Finch: Adult; Caleta Black, Isabela, Galápagos; August 1995; Andy Swash.
Warbler Finch: Adult cinerascens; Española, Galápagos; August 1995; Andy Swash.
Warbler Finch: Adult mentalis; Genovesa, Galápagos; August 1995; Andy Swash.
Warbler Finch: Adult olivacea; Santa Cruz, Galápagos; May 1997; Bruce Hallett.
Woodpecker Finch: Adult non-breeding; Isabela, Galápagos; August 1995; Andy Swash.
Woodpecker Finch: Adult, breeding; Santa Cruz, Galápagos; August 1995; Andy Swash.

The reptiles of Galápagos
Page 110. **Galápagos (or Giant) Tortoise:** Adult; Santa Cruz, Galápagos; August 1995; Andy Swash.
Page 111. **Black (or Pacific Green) Turtle:** Adult; Santa Cruz, Galápagos; January 1996; Andy Swash.
Page 111. **Galápagos Lava Lizard:** Adult male; South Plaza, Galápagos; January 1996; Andy Swash.
Page 111. **Marine Iguana:** Adult male; Isabela, Galápagos; January 1996; Andy Swash.
Page 112. **Galápagos Leaf-toed Gecko:** Adult; Galápagos; Source of photo unknown despite best endeavours.
Page 112. **Española Snake:** Adult; Española, Galápagos; David Horwell.
Page 112. **Yellow-bellied (or Pelagic) Sea Snake:** Adult; Costa Rica; Phil Myers/Animal Diversity Web.

The reptile plates
The species listed for each plate are shown in alphabetical order:

Plate 39
Galápagos (or Giant) Tortoise: Adult hoodensis; captive, Charles Darwin Research Station, Santa Cruz, Galápagos; August 1995; Andy Swash.
Galápagos (or Giant) Tortoise: Adult porteri; Santa Cruz, Galápagos; August 1995; Andy Swash.
Galápagos (or Giant) Tortoise carapaces; drawings by Rob Still after PRITCHARD, C. H. (1979) Encyclopaedia of Turtles.

Plate 40
Black (or Pacific Green) Turtle: Adult female on beach; Bartolomé, Galápagos; January 1996; Andy Swash.
Black (or Pacific Green), Hawksbill, Leatherback and Olive Ridley Turtles carapaces and heads: Illustrations by Rob Still.

Plate 41
Land Iguana: Adult; South Plaza, Galápagos; January 1996; Andy Swash.
Land Iguana: Adult; South Plaza, Galápagos; January 1996; Andy Swash.
Marine Iguana: Adult male ssp. *venustissimus*; Española, Galápagos; January 1996; Andy Swash.
Marine Iguana: Adult male ssp. *cristatus*; Fernandina, Galápagos; January 1996; Andy Swash.
Marine Iguana: Adult male ssp. *albemarlensis*; Isabela, Galápagos; January 1996; Andy Swash.
Marine Iguana: Group of females ssp. *cristatus*; Fernandina, Galápagos; August 1995; Andy Swash.
Marine Iguana: Females ssp. *hassi*; South Plaza, Galápagos; August 1995; Andy Swash.
Marine x Land Iguana hybrid: Subadult; South Plaza, Galápagos; David Horwell.
Santa Fé Land Iguana: Adult; Santa Fé, Galápagos; January 1996; Andy Swash.
Santa Fé Land Iguana: Adult; Santa Fé, Galápagos; January 1996; Andy Swash.

Plate 42
Española Lava Lizard: Female; Española, Galápagos; August 1995; Andy Swash.
Española Lava Lizard: Male; Española, Galápagos; January 1996; Andy Swash.
Floreana Lava Lizard: Male; Gardner-near-Floreana, Galápagos; July 1999; Heidi Snell.
Galápagos Lava Lizard: Female; South Plaza, Galápagos; August 1995; Andy Swash.
Galápagos Lava Lizard: Immature; South Plaza, Galápagos; August 1997; Phil Hansbro.
Galápagos Lava Lizard: Male; South Plaza, Galápagos; January 1996; Andy Swash.
Marchena Lava Lizard: Male; Marchena, Galápagos; August 1998; Heidi Snell.
Pinzón Lava Lizard: Female; Pinzon, Galápagos; June 2000; Heidi Snell.
San Cristóbal Lava Lizard: Male; Isla Lobos, Galápagos; July 1987; Howard Snell.

Plate 43
Galápagos Leaf-toed Gecko: Adult; Isla Tortuga, Galápagos; 1999; Heidi Snell.
Galápagos Leaf-toed Gecko: Adult on lava; Galápagos; Source of photo unknown despite best endeavours.
Galápagos Leaf-toed Gecko: Adult on stones; Galápagos; David Horwell.
Gecko *Lepidodactylus lugubris*: Adult; captive; Boris Klusmeyer/Global Gecko Association.

Plate 44
Española Snake: Adult; Española, Galápagos; David Horwell.
Fernandina Snake: Adult; Fernandina, Galápagos; August 1995; Andy Swash.
Steindachner's Snake: Adult; Santa Cruz, Galápagos; David Horwell.
Yellow bellied (or Pelagic) Sea Snake: Adult; Costa Rica; Phil Myers/Animal Diversity Web.

The mammals of Galápagos

Page 126. Galápagos Fur Seal: Female; Santiago, Galápagos; August 1995; Andy Swash.
Page 126. Large Fernandina Rice Rat: Fernandina, Galápagos; Robert C. Dowler.
Page 127. Galápagos Red Bat: San Cristóbal, Galápagos; Gary F. McCracken.
Page 128. Blue Whale: Blow; Snaefellsness, Iceland; June 1998; Dylan Walker.
Page 128. Humpback Whale: Breaching; Maui, Hawaii, USA; March 1996; Lori Mazzuca.
Page 128. Northern Bottlenose Whale: Spy-hopping; Skye, Scotland; August 1998: Dylan Walker.
Page 128. Humpback Whale: Fluking; Keflavik, Iceland; June 1998; Dylan Walker.
Page 129. Blue Whale and head: illustration by Marc Dando from Sealife: A Guide to the Marine Environment (ed. G. Waller), Pica Press, UK.
Page 129. Striped Dolphin: illustration by Marc Dando from Sealife: A Guide to the Marine Environment (ed. G. Waller), Pica Press, UK.
Page 129. Short-finned Pilot Whales: Logging; Tenerife; September 1998; Dylan Walker.
Page 129. Dusky Dolphin and Common Dolphin: Porpoising; Kaikoura, New Zealand; March 1999; Sam Taylor.
Page 130. Blue Whale: Snaefellsness, Iceland; June 1998; Dylan Walker.
Page 130. Sperm Whale: Manado, North Sulawesi, Indonesia; August 1998, Pietro Pecchioni.
Page 130. Blainville's Beaked Whale: Hope Town, Bahamas; March 1994; Stephanie A. Norman.
Page 130. Short-finned Pilot Whale: Tenerife; February 1998; Dylan Walker.
Page 131. Long-snouted Spinner Dolphin: Maui, Hawaii, USA; February 1998; Lori Mazzuca.

The mammal plates
The species listed for each plate are shown in alphabetical order:

Plate 45
Galápagos Fur Seal: Female with pup; Santiago, Galápagos; August 1995; Andy Swash.
Galápagos Fur Seal: Bull; Galápagos; David Horwell.
Galápagos Sea Lion: Bull; Galápagos; David Horwell.
Galápagos Sea Lion: Females; Genovesa, Galápagos; August 1995; Andy Swash.
Galápagos Sea Lion: Pup; Santiago, Galápagos, August 1995; Andy Swash.

Plate 46
Large Fernandina Rice Rat: Fernandina, Galápagos; Robert C. Dowler.
Small Fernandina Rice Rat: Fernandina, Galápagos; Robert C. Dowler.
Santa Fé Rice Rat: Santa Fé, Galápagos; 1980; Howard Snell.
Santiago Rice Rat: Santiago, Galápagos; Cody W. Edwards.

Plate 47
Black Rat: Mark Lucas.
Brown Rat: Colin Carver.
Galápagos Red Bat: San Cristóbal, Galápagos; Gary F. McCracken.
Hoary Bat: Isabela, Galápagos; Gary F. McCracken.
House Mouse: Richard Revels.

Plate 48
Bryde's Whale: Back and dorsal fin; Maldives; Alex Carlisle.
Bryde's Whale: Blow; Maldives; Charles Anderson.
Bryde's Whale: Head: Gran Canaria; Graeme Cresswell.
Fin Whale: Back and dorsal fin; Monterey Bay, California, USA; August 1997; Graeme Cresswell.
Fin Whale: Blowhole and blow; Bay of Fundy, Canada; August 1998; Graeme Cresswell.
Fin Whale: Left jaw; Gulf of St. Lawrence, Canada; August 1998; Graeme Cresswell.
Fin Whale: Right jaw; Gulf of St. Lawrence, Canada; August 1998; Graeme Cresswell.
Minke Whale: Back and dorsal fin; Gulf of St. Lawrence, Canada; August 1998; Graeme Cresswell.
Sei Whale: Back and dorsal fin; Stephen Wong.
Sei Whale: Blow; Stephen Wong.

Plate 49
Blue Whale: Back and dorsal fin; Snaefellsness, Iceland; June 1998; Graeme Cresswell.
Blue Whale: Blow; Snaefellsness, Iceland; June 1998; Dylan Walker.
Humpback Whale: Back and dorsal fin; Keflavik, Iceland; June 1998; Dylan Walker.
Humpback Whale: Pair surfacing; Keflavik, Iceland; June 1998; Graeme Cresswell.
Humpback Whale: Tail; Maui, Hawaii, USA; February 1996; Lori Mazzuca.
Sperm Whale: Blow: Kaikoura, New Zealand; April 1999; Sam Taylor.
Sperm Whale: Head and back; Bay of Biscay; August 2002; Hugh Harrop.
Sperm Whale: Tail; Kaikoura, New Zealand; January 1999; Sam Taylor.

Plate 50
Blainville's Beaked Whale: Back and dorsal fin; The Bahamas; 2000; C. D. Macleod.
Blainville's Beaked Whale: Head; The Bahamas; 2000; C. D. Macleod.
Cuvier's Beaked Whale: Female; North Carolina, USA; 2001; Graeme Cresswell.
Cuvier's Beaked Whale: Head; North Carolina, USA; 2001; Graeme Cresswell.

Cuvier's Beaked Whale: Male; Bay of Biscay, Spain; 2002; Matt Hobbs.
Dwarf Sperm Whale: Manado, North Sulawesi, Indonesia; August 1998; Pietro Pecchioni.
Pygmy Sperm Whale: Robert L. Pitman.

Plate 51
False Killer Whale: Surfacing; 1998; Peggy Stap.
Killer Whale (or Orca): Female; Snaefellsness, Iceland; June 1998; Graeme Cresswell.
Killer Whale (or Orca): Adult male; Kaikoura, New Zealand; January 1999; Sam Taylor.
Melon-headed Whale: Group; Lana'i, Hawaii, USA; October 1997; Lori Mazzuca.
Melon-headed Whale: Head; The Bahamas; 2000; C. D. Macleod.
Melon-headed Whale: Spy-hopping; Manado, North Sulawesi, Indonesia; June 1998; Carla Benoldi.
Pygmy Killer Whale: Head; Off New South Wales, Australia; Simon Mustoe.
Short-finned Pilot Whale: Group; Tenerife; October 1998; Dylan Walker.
Short-finned Pilot Whale: Head; Tenerife; October 1998; Dylan Walker.

Plate 52
Common Dolphin: Porpoising; Mercury Bay, New Zealand; March 1999; Dirk Neumann.
Long-snouted Spinner Dolphin: Porpoising; Gulf of Mexico, Dagmar C. Fertl.
Pantropical Spotted Dolphin: Porpoising; Ecuador; November 1998; Stephanie A. Norman.
Striped Dolphin: Porpoising; Gulf of Mexico; Dagmar C. Fertl.

Plate 53
Bottle-nosed Dolphin: Surfacing; Tenerife; October 1998; Dylan Walker.
Fraser's Dolphin: Robert L. Pitman/Seapics.com.
Risso's Dolphin: Pair surfacing; Manado, North Sulawesi, Indonesia; September 1998; Carla Benoldi.
Rough-toothed Dolphin: Breaching; Tahiti; May 1999; Sam Taylor.

If you believe you have better quality photos of any of the species in this guide please contact the authors at the **WILD**Guides address or email photos@wildguides.co.uk

INDEX OF ENGLISH AND SCIENTIFIC NAMES

This index includes the common English and scientific names of all the birds, mammals and reptiles mentioned in the text.

Figures in *italicised bold red text* refer to the number(s) of the plate(s) on which the species is illustrated.

Figures in *italicised bold black text* indicate other page number(s) on which there is an illustration.

Figures in **bold text** refer to the page(s) on which the main text for the species can be found.

Figures in plain text relate to other page(s) where the species is mentioned.